# BETTER BUSINESS MEETINGS

*Robert B. Nelson*

*Peter Economy*

*Professional Publishing*
Burr Ridge, Illinois
New York, New York

The Briefcase Books Series

Managing Stress: Keeping Calm Under Fire
*Barbara J. Braham*

Business Negotiating Basics
*Peter Economy*

Straight Answers to People Problems
*Fred E. Jandt*

Empowering Employees through Delegation
*Robert B. Nelson*

The Presentation Primer: Getting Your Point Across
*Robert B. Nelson*
*Jennifer Wallick*

Listen for Success: A Guide to Effective Listening
*Arthur K. Robertson*

The New Manager's Handbook
*Brad Thompson*

# The Briefcase Books Series

Research shows that people who buy business books (1) want books that can be read quickly, perhaps on a plane trip, commuting on a train, or overnight, and (2) feel their time and money were well spent if they get two or three useful insights or techniques for improving their professional skills or helping them with a current problem at work.

Briefcase Books were designed to meet these two criteria. They focus on necessary skills and problem areas, and include real-world examples from practicing managers and professionals. Inside these books you'll find useful, practical information and techniques in a straightforward, concise, and easy-to-read format.

This book and others like it in the Briefcase Books series can quickly give you insights and answers regarding your current needs and problems. And they are useful references for future situations and problems.

If you find this book or any other in this series to be of value, please share it with your co-workers. With tens of thousands of new books published each year, any book that can simplify the growing complexities in managing others needs to be circulated as widely as possible.

**Robert B. Nelson**
**Series Editor**

Senior sponsoring editor:     Cynthia A. Zigmund
Project editor:               Becky Dodson
Interior designer:            Heidi J. Baughman
Cover designer:               Tim Kaage
Art manager:                  Kim Meriwether
Compositor:                   Wm. C. Brown Communications, Inc.
Typeface:                     11/13 Palatino
Printer:                      Book Press, Inc.

**Library of Congress Cataloging-in-Publication Data**

Nelson, Robert B.
Better business meetings / Robert B. Nelson, Peter Economy.
p. cm.—(Briefcase books series)
Includes index.
ISBN 0–7863–0188–0.—ISBN 0–7863–0205–4 (pbk.)
1. Meetings.   2. Business communication.   I. Economy, Peter.
II. Title.   III. Series.
HF5734.5.N45   1995
658.4'56—dc20                                            94–9330

*Printed in the United States of America*

2 3 4 5 6 7 8 9 0 BP 1 0 9 8 7 6 5 4

*To our children: Daniel Edward Nelson and*
*Skylar Park Economy (the girl of my dreams)*

# Foreword

My mission in life has been to be a conveyor of simple truths. It is for that reason that I'm pleased to be able to introduce the Briefcase Books series, which seeks to provide simple, practical, and direct answers to the most common problems managers face on a daily basis.

It has been my experience that in the field of business common sense is not common practice. So it is refreshing to find a series of books that glorifies common sense in dealing with people in the workplace.

Take the skill of listening. We all know that it is important to listen, yet how many of us actually do it well? I suggest it would be rare to find one in a hundred managers who is truly a good listener. Most people focus on what they are going to say next when someone else is talking. They would seldom if ever think to check what they thought they heard to make sure it is accurate. And they seldom acknowledge or attempt to deal with emotions when they occur in speaking with someone at work. These are basic errors in the use of this basic skill. And regardless of how much education or experience you have, you should know how to listen.

But how much training have you had on the topic of listening? Have you ever had a course on the topic? Have you ever tested your ability to listen? Have you ever discussed with others how you could listen better with greater comprehension and respect? Probably not. Even though this fundamental interpersonal skill could cripple the most talented individual if he or she is not good at it.

Fortunately, listening is just one of the fundamental skills singled out for its own volume in the Briefcase Books series. Others include books on making presentations, negotiating, problem solving, and handling stress. And other volumes are planned even as I write this.

The Briefcase Books series focuses on those basic skills that managers must master to excel at work. Whether you are new to managing or are a seasoned manager, you'll find these books of value in obtaining useful insights and fundamental knowledge you can use for your entire career.

**Ken Blanchard**
**Co-author**
*The One Minute Manager*

# Preface

The importance of knowing how to conduct an effective business meeting cannot be understated. Besieged by non-stop changes and fundamental shifts of operating assumptions, today's managers must continually return to the basics of effective management, communication, and decision making. Nowhere are these basics better exemplified than in the format of face-to-face meetings.

Anyone who has spent even a nominal amount of time involved with business meetings knows that the challenge of making this vehicle effective is daunting. The sheer number of meetings most people attend is overwhelming. The fact that about half of all meeting time is reportedly wasted comes as little surprise. But the ultimate blow to the medium is the damning report that even the time not completely wasted tends to be unproductive.

This book tackles these problems head on. It introduces an especially effective meeting management tool, the concept of Power Dynamics, in which every person in attendance accepts the responsibility of being an active participant and advocate, rather than a passive observer. We will show you how to engage meeting attendees even before they come to the session, how to focus dispersed energy on a single productive purpose, and how to clearly define the roles of meeting leader and meeting participant.

We may be stuck with meetings as a fact of organizational life but, with this book, no one has to any longer accept being a bystander to ineffectiveness in the meetings they attend.

**Robert B. Nelson**
San Diego, California

**Peter Economy**
Pacific Beach, California

# Acknowledgments

Special thanks to Cafe Crema, Pacific Beach, California, for the swirling, caffeine-laden atmosphere that was so conducive to the flow of words from pen to paper; Cathy Lexin for being such a great boss (now, about that raise . . .); *Strawberry Fields Forever* for changing *my* life forever; Debbie Fritsch for all the great discussions over lunch (whose turn is it to pick up the tab?); *very* late nights with Mahler's Fifth (especially the synapse-shattering Rondo-Finale: Allegro), Smashing Pumpkins, *and* Frank Zappa; Maria Elena Goldman for *grande* mocha espresso runs to Starbucks (¡Cuba libre!); John Chase, Yinka Adesanwo, Patricia Wilson, and the rest of the General Services staff for their superb efforts and support; my co-author Robert B. Nelson for many, many years of friendship and a level of understanding that transcends the bonds of mere conscious thought and existence (could *anyone* in this universe have a friendship deeper than ours?); my mother, Betty, for *always* being there when I needed her (you'll never know how much I love you); and, of course, my wife Jan (who I love more than life itself)—for midnight sashimi-fests and countless *kampai* with bottomless sake cups, for memories of Tahitian *motus* and Hawaiian cliffs, for making me smile, and for bringing our two beautiful children, Peter J and Skylar Park into my life. *May the circle be unbroken.*

# Contents

*Chapter One*
THE INCREASED IMPORTANCE OF     1
MEETINGS IN TODAY'S ORGANIZATIONS

The Competitive Climate, 3
The Need for Active Communication, 6
Advantages of Meetings, 9

*Chapter Two*
WHY MEETINGS FAIL     12

Too Many Meetings, 14
Meetings Take Too Much Time, 16
Meetings Are Inefficient and Unproductive, 17
Lack of Preparation, 20
Too Many Egos, 21
Too Few Lions, 24
You Get What You Reward, 25

*Chapter Three*
WHY MEET?     27

Reasons to Meet, 28
Goals of Group Meetings, 30
Who, Why, and How Many?, 31
Scheduling, 34
Set Ground Rules for All Participants, 36
Preparing an Agenda, 42
How to Have Fewer Meetings, 45

*Chapter Four*
MEETING MANAGEMENT TOOLS                          50

Power Dynamics Planning, 51
Who Has a Critical Contribution?, 52
Drawing Out Minority Opinion, 56
Using Power Dynamics to Change Group
Behavior, 57
When and How to Conclude, 67
Feedback Mechanisms and Evaluation, 69

*Chapter Five*
MEETING LEADERSHIP                                72

What Is Group Leadership?, 73
Myths of Leadership, 75
Key Leadership Skills, 79
How to Encourage Input, 83
Ways to Control Discussion, 85
Share the Wealth, 90
Build a Team, 93

*Chapter Six*
THE ROLE OF PARTICIPANTS                          95

Each Member as Leader, 96
Key Participant Skills, 98
How to Effectively Influence Groups, 104
How to Disagree, 109

*Chapter Seven*
MISTAKES TO AVOID WHEN MEETING    112

Getting Off the Subject, 113
No Goals, No Agenda, 115
Meeting Too Long, 117

Lack of Preparation, 120
Ambiguous Results, 123
Key Players Missing in Action, 127
Dictatorship of the Few, 128

*Chapter Eight*
VALUING OUR DIFFERENCES                    130

The Good Old Boys, 131
The Nature of Our Differences, 134
Meeting Techniques That Capture and Value
Our Differences, 140
Pseudo-Inclusionary Tactics, 142
Gaining a Competitive Advantage, 147
How to Tap the Full Potential of the
Organization, 150

*Chapter Nine*
THE LEADING EDGE OF MEETINGS          155

Employee Empowerment, 156
Quality Circles, 159
Self-Managing Work Teams, 161
Electronic Meetings, 166
Decision Support Systems, 169

*Chapter Ten*
BETTER BUSINESS MEETINGS                   171

*Endnotes, 174*
*Index, 176*

## Chapter 1

# The Increased Importance of Meetings in Today's Organizations

**Objectives:**

- To explain that the accelerating pace of our modern society has increased the demand for communication in organizations.
- To describe the advantages of active forms of communication over passive forms of communication.
- To show how meetings can help us to better manage the increasingly complex and rapid flows of information from outside and within an organization.

We live in a fast-paced world. A little over one hundred years ago, it took a Pony Express rider five days to deliver a letter from St. Louis, Missouri, to Sacramento, California. Today, the Federal Express Corporation routinely delivers thousands of letters and parcels along the same route—and halfway around the world—overnight.

With the near real-time information transmission of our present-day global media network, and with the advent of

1

24-hour television news sources such as CNN, the Cable News Network, it's quite possible to be aware of any significant event worldwide only minutes after its occurrence.

By way of contrast, in the early days of the American republic, it took days or weeks for news to travel from city to city or colony to colony. Because of the difficulty and relative slowness of communication in the years preceding the advent of electricity, the telegraph, and radio, the greatest battle of the War of 1812, the Battle of New Orleans, took place two weeks after the war officially ended.

In business, we rely on the quick transmission of information to maintain our competitive edge. We need to know everything, and we need to know it right now. Yesterday isn't good enough anymore.

From time immemorial, the basic reasons for having meetings have been fairly constant: to make decisions and to communicate information. With the colossal increase in the speed of communication within the last two decades, and with the tremendous increase in the diversity, size, and complexity of business organizations and of the entire global business environment, meetings have become more important than ever as an aid to fostering the health, welfare, and competitive edge of every organization. In recent years, however, meetings have fallen well short of the mark.

More and more business professionals are reporting that they spend more time in meetings, but that the effectiveness of the time spent has actually decreased. In many cases, we delay decisions *ad infinitum* as we postpone meetings or allow them to meander aimlessly with no agenda or direction. We delay decisions further with the appointment of subcommittees that then create their own cycles of dysfunctional behavior. Some meetings end in utter shambles as we make decisions by default—not by group consensus. Finally, some participants just give up on the meeting process altogether and make their decisions outside the meeting.

J. Peter Grace, CEO of W. R. Grace, the chemical and health care powerhouse, is a vocal critic of meetings. Quoted in an article in *Fortune* magazine, Grace states, "I consider meetings major time wasters. I try to avoid them at all costs."[1] While J. Peter Grace might be able to avoid meetings, his organization cannot. Grace's solution to the meeting dilemma is to let his subordinates hold meetings and then report the results back to him.

## THE COMPETITIVE CLIMATE

During the height of the economic expansion of the 80s, whoever thought we would see the severe economic decline of the 90s? With this decline, organizations have had to become much more competitive to stay alive. By now, you have no doubt heard the bleating of management consultants and gurus of the latest business fads:

❏ The customer is king.
❏ Speed is life.
❏ Total quality management.
❏ Employee empowerment.
❏ Process re-engineering.

These are the buzzwords of American organizations that are frantically, no, desperately, trying to find any advantage possible to stay ahead of the competition.

Call it what you want, the simple fact is if you are not actively pursuing ways to cut your costs and make your organization more efficient, you are falling behind your competition. In this fast-paced world, simply keeping up is no longer good enough. Like the dodo birds whose wings were utterly useless for flight, the static organizations of the past are destined for extinction—no matter how large or how powerful they might be. To survive, every organization must constantly and aggressively seek out ways to stay a step ahead of the competition.

To help organizations digest and handle the implications and impact of today's rapidly changing business environment, meetings have become more important than ever as a vehicle for communication, decision making, and problem solving, as well as a tool to help manage the change process within organizations. While there are many other means of communication within an organization—memos, videotapes, electronic mail, and so forth—few can approach the effectiveness of a *well-run* meeting.

The practice of many organizations of maintaining the status quo and wasting precious people's resources, and the upward spiraling costs of doing business in today's environment have exacerbated the problem of ineffective meetings. Unfortunately, most of us do little more than talk about the problem—few of us appreciate the full extent of the problem in our organizations or the tremendous cost to our bottom lines. Still fewer of us have any idea of what to do to solve the problem of ineffective meetings—even if we were predisposed to do so.

Regardless of our respective abilities or inabilities to address the problems with meetings, the facts are simple and compelling:

❑ *The number of meetings we attend is increasing.* The frequency of meetings has continued to grow over the years. As communication gets faster and faster, meetings help us keep up. All indications are that meeting frequency will continue its upward surge in the future.

❏ *The average business person spends over 25 percent of his or her time in meetings.* Middle managers and technical professionals average two days per week in meetings, while it is not uncommon for high-level managers to spend up to four days a week in meetings, not including impromptu meetings. It's not surprising that many of us feel we spend all our time in meetings and precious little time doing our jobs—because it's true!

❏ *Over 50 percent of our meeting time is wasted.* Research has shown that meeting efficiency averages 47 percent. In other words, for every hour we spend in meetings, roughly half an hour is wasted. Every year, American organizations waste billions of otherwise productive hours in inefficient and ineffective meetings.

❏ *This hidden drain on American industry threatens our economic future.* It only makes sense that the increasingly large number of hours wasted each year in business meetings has a negative impact on the ability of our economy to become competitive in the world market. An environment that allows a firm with 50,000 employees to lose in excess of 10 million worker-hours a year due to inefficient and ineffective meetings is one that makes it nearly impossible for our nation to regain its economic footing.

Of course, whether or not we choose to conduct or participate in meetings, the frenetic pace that we all constantly endure shows no signs of abating. If anything, with future advances in technology, we can only expect the pace of business to continue to increase. We can therefore also expect the demand for meetings to continue to increase in our organizations, as we all try to stay on top of the swiftly flowing waters of change.

While many of us complain about meetings—their length, their frequency, their outcomes—we can all expect to spend much of our future careers deeply immersed in them. Despite the very real problems with meetings, they are still the best way to draw together a team of people to solve an urgent problem, deliberate a complex set of facts, or communicate important organizational information. Our task, then, in a rapidly changing organization and in a rapidly changing world is to commit ourselves to applying the most effective, state-of-the-art methods for better managing our meetings. We can no longer tolerate the very real waste of time and resources that ill-conceived and poorly run meetings incur.

For years, many of us have simply stuck our heads in the sand and allowed ourselves to be passive participants in meetings, or have actually conducted meetings that, through their sheer ineffectiveness, were slowly but surely sucking the lifeblood out of our organizations. Far too few of us have been willing to put a stop to this silent killer. It's now time for us to do something positive about it. By doing so, we can ensure that we are leaders of change in our organizations.

## THE NEED FOR ACTIVE COMMUNICATION

Meetings are an essential part of our organizational lives—whether we like that fact or not. When there is a problem that needs fixing, we call a meeting. When we communicate new information in an organization, we can ensure that the message is received by all team members by announcing the information in a meeting. When it is time for us to review the progress of those who work for us, the preferred forum is a meeting.

The memorandum is one example of information synthesis that generally misses the mark. While a memo is an active, participative event for the author, it is a passive, uninvolved event for the recipient. And, while the general aim of the writer of the memo is to elicit support for an idea, or generate some amount of agreement on a topic within a group, memos are inherently inefficient and bureaucratic, and tend to be a part of the miles and miles of red tape that constrain and confound most organizations.

The following example describes exactly what we are talking about. A manager spent days agonizing over the exact wording of a memorandum recommending changes to the corporate policy on expense reporting. Not wanting to offend his boss, the manager made sure that every word was just right before he finalized the memo and sent it out through interdepartmental mail.

Approximately four weeks later, a new policy on expense reporting was distributed throughout the corporation. Our manager read through the new policy—anxiously anticipating the incorporation of his insights. To his utter surprise, the policy bore no resemblance whatsoever to the ideas he'd outlined in his memo to his boss. Thinking that perhaps his memo had been misplaced, the manager called his boss to find out what happened to it.

**✱ ✱ ✱ ✱ ✱**

"So, Debbie, I just received the new policy on expense reporting. I'm kind of surprised by the final wording of the policy."

"What's that, Pat? Why would the wording of the policy surprise you?"

"Well, Debbie, it's just that I sent you a memo a month ago with some pretty detailed suggestions for a new policy, but I don't see any of them in the final version."

"Memo? What memo? Oh, wait a minute. I remember. I read your memo and had a few questions. I got so busy with the DVI proposal that I forgot all about it. Deirdre stopped by my office a couple of weeks ago and bounced some ideas off of me. I told her to take the ball and run with it."

**✱ ✱ ✱ ✱ ✱**

In the above example, the author was very much an active part of the memorandum. His boss, however, was not. The end result was that the manager who drafted the memo did not achieve his goals. In this particular case, it clearly would have been better if he had scheduled a brief meeting with his boss to make his points and then suggested a plan for acting on them. Instead, the memorandum fell flat, and the hours that Pat spent agonizing over its wording were a total waste of time.

---

If you wish to avoid making a decision, either send a memo . . . or set up a committee to conduct an indepth study.

—*Epson's Compleat Office Companion*

---

Despite our best intentions, any communication that is in written instead of verbal form is going to suffer in the translation. We have seen many situations where co-workers misconstrued the tone or contents of a memorandum, at the expense of the point being made. The problem is that, once a writer drafts and mails out a memo, he or she loses control of the message. The writer of the memo may or may not be around to explain his or her intent to the recipient. In the case where the recipient draws an erroneous or incorrect conclusion, the only result may be confusion, resentment or outright hostility and rebellion. Instead of helping to unify and synthesize information flows, memos, when improperly utilized, may have the actual result of destroying and subverting information flows.

Meetings, on the other hand, when effectively conducted, can be much more efficient than written communication. If the recipient of the information is unclear about the intent or content of the information, you can resolve the issue in real time right then and there.

While memos have their place, there are several important human elements of communication in meetings that memoranda just cannot provide. First, meetings allow for questions and answers and additional clarifications as needed. Second, they allow for the next step or action to be taken as a result of a common understanding and discussion of the situation at hand.

## ADVANTAGES OF MEETINGS

While there are countless ways to communicate within an organization, none of these ways are as versatile as the meeting. While the meeting format offers many advantages, the key advantages of meetings are their flexibility and their adaptability.

We can schedule a meeting with only a moment's notice, or months in advance, depending on the priority of the issue. We can adapt schedules, and we can advance or slip times to meet the needs of all participants. And, if the need for the meeting no longer exists, we can cancel the meeting.

Attendance in a meeting is fully adaptable to the nature of the issue at hand and the needs of the organization. When it comes to holding a meeting, the possibilities are endless. Anyone from the chairman of the board to the guy helping in the mailroom can potentially be invited. Depending on the particular issue, that guy in the mailroom may know a lot more about what's really happening in the organization than the chairman!

Meetings can be held anywhere: in a conference room, an office, or even in the hallway or parking lot. Meetings can be held on-site or off-site and they can be, and often are, held at secluded resorts or other hideaways. It's only when large numbers of people attend meetings that location can become an issue.

If you control the agenda, you can decide exactly what topics you will address. So, what exactly is an agenda, and how do you draft one that will help you best achieve your goals? An agenda is nothing more than a list of the topics you want to discuss during the course of your meeting. There is nothing magical or mystical about the use of an agenda in a meeting. The agenda simply becomes a compass to help guide the leader and participants through the potentially hazardous brambles and pitfalls of the typical business meeting. If you're not satisfied with the direction or progress of discussion during the course of the meeting, you can redirect it. Furthermore, you can add or delete topics at will, or change the entire direction of a meeting in midstream.

For example, you may have initiated a meeting to discuss one particular issue, say, the continuing problem of payroll errors. Part way into the meeting, you may discover that the errors are not a result of the payroll department, but of processing problems with your bank. On the basis of that discovery, you can immediately redirect the meeting to explore problems with the bank instead of the payroll department. You can even send the payroll representatives back to their department and call in the people within your organization who deal directly with the bank.

Finally, many organizations talk a good story about teamwork and employee empowerment, but few actually walk their talk. Meetings offer a tremendous opportunity for organizations to include their employees in the decision process and, at the same time, solicit ideas from those employees who know the most about their piece of the business. There are decisions that employees can make within the lower reaches of the organizational hierarchy— even in the most dictatorial firm. It should be the task of every supervisor or manager to identify these decisions and include all levels of staff in the decision-making process where relevant.

The rewards in productivity, improved staff morale, and team cohesion are worth their weight in gold. Wise supervisors or managers will take advantage of every possible opportunity to use meetings to help them achieve their goals.

In the chapters that follow, we will introduce you to many meeting techniques and concepts that you can quickly, easily, and effectively apply within your own organization. Some of the techniques have been around for years. Others, however, such as the idea of Power Dynamics, are new, and more innovative.

Regardless of which approaches you choose to take, we are certain that, after reading this book and applying the techniques presented herein, you will find your future meetings to be much more efficient, meaningful, and productive.

*Chapter 2*

# Why Meetings Fail

**Objectives:**

- To identify and describe the most common reasons why meetings fail.
- To explore the very real cost of failed meetings to organizations.
- To briefly describe some simple strategies for making meetings successful.

Unfortunately, many meetings are doomed to failure. Despite our best efforts to make them successful, the majority of business meetings are both inefficient and ineffective. Many managers have spent a lot of time and money trying to improve their business meetings—only to find that they are little better than before. Other managers have found it easier to try to avoid meetings altogether. How can it be that this most important of management tools could fail so often and so abysmally?

According to *Fortune* magazine, after returning from a nine-week sabbatical in Maine, John Sculley, recently of Apple Computer, was ready to ban all business meetings within the corporation. Why was he ready to banish meetings from the Apple corporate suites?

✳ ✳ ✳ ✳ ✳

"I think I got a lot more done in Maine with my link to Apple through electronic mail, facsimile, and Federal Express than I would have sitting in meetings back in Silicon Valley. If we could ban meetings as a form of management, American productivity would probably go up."[1]

✳ ✳ ✳ ✳ ✳

Despite our aversion to meetings, they have become indispensable, albeit inefficient, tools for coordinating complex and interdependent organizational elements and for bringing together a project team or pooling information or talent.

This leaves most managers with only a few options. We can choose to continue to conduct meetings—hoping that the benefits will at least partially offset the costs of inefficient meeting practices. Or we can choose to shun the use of meetings except when absolutely necessary. While this option avoids the negative effects of inefficient meetings on an organization, it fails to take advantage of the many positive reasons for conducting a well-run and efficient meeting. Finally, we can choose to confront the problem of ineffective meetings head on and take steps to make them more efficient and more effective.

The first option is, unfortunately, the path most often selected by managers. Instead of learning and applying techniques to improve their meetings, managers often find themselves so caught up fighting fires that they have precious little time available to devote to planning ahead or improving their personal business skills.

The second option is generally not available to most business people. Few individuals are truly independent of an organization to the extent that they can avoid meetings. There may, of course, be a few disgruntled lone wolves lurking in the hidden recesses of an organization, but their impact on the organization will be proportionally limited and lacking in import. In today's organizations, knowledge and information equal power and, increasingly, those who avoid meetings, and who avoid getting on board with electronic and voice mail, are relegated to the ash heap of corporate history.

The third option is obviously the preferred one. It is, unfortunately, the least pursued by most business people. Instead of learning new ways to make meetings succeed, too many of us continue to follow timeworn patterns of meeting management that lead to the failure of our business meetings and do far more to harm our organizations than most of us suspect.

There are probably just about as many reasons behind the failure of meetings as there are stars in the sky. The following are most often cited by managers:

❑ Too many meetings.
❑ Meetings take too much time.
❑ Meetings are often inefficient and unproductive.

Let's take some time to closely examine the most common reasons for the failure of business meetings. As you read the sections that follow, see if you can think of examples of poorly run meetings from your own personal experience. If you are like most business people, you should have no trouble coming up with plenty of examples that illustrate the continuing problems that we all have with meeting management.

## TOO MANY MEETINGS

I sincerely doubt that you will find anyone in any organization who says that they don't participate in enough meetings. On the contrary, most of us feel that, due to the excessive number of meetings we attend, we don't have enough time to get our real work done. More often than not, this is not just a feeling, but a very real fact.

In too many organizations, we call meetings to deal with every little crisis—no matter how small or how trivial. Some people feel that every problem requires a group process to solve. Not only is this often an inefficient use of scarce company resources, but it is often an ineffective way to deal with simple issues.

Having more meetings doesn't necessarily lead to more or better solutions. In fact, the converse is often the case. Within every organization, we reach a point where additional meetings hinder productive work. This is especially true when large numbers of key employees are regularly drawn away from their regular work to attend meetings that may or may not be of importance to them.

How many times have you attended a meeting, listened politely for a while, and then wondered to yourself: "What *am* I doing here?" If you experience this unique sensation more than once or twice a month, it's a sure sign of an organization that has too many meetings.

Schedule meetings only when absolutely necessary. Just because the issue is important to you doesn't necessarily mean that the issue has equal importance to those whom you invite to attend. Before you schedule your next meeting, ask yourself if there isn't some other way of resolving the issue. Would a phone call do? Or, perhaps just five minutes of face-to-face time with a co-worker in her office?

Remember, the power to call a meeting carries with it the responsibility to ensure that it is an effective use of time for all participants instead of a big waste of time. The next time you find yourself in a meeting, take a look around and make a mental note of which participants are really involved, and which participants are just spinning their wheels. Use this information to make adjustments to your future meetings.

## MEETINGS TAKE TOO MUCH TIME

Compounding the problem of too many meetings is the fact that meetings often take far longer than necessary to fully address and resolve an issue. Instead of having the courage to take the initiative to end a meeting when they resolve an issue or when it is obvious that no solution is in sight, many participants will continue to meet until they exhaust the time allotted by the schedule or agenda. Only then does everyone feel comfortable with ending the meeting.

While there are many reasons to end a meeting, we can summarize them in the following rule:

| |
|---|
| End the meeting the moment the objectives are achieved or when progress towards meeting them ceases. |

Imagine for a moment that management sent your entire department out of town for a three-day meeting. Your organization has gone to great pains and expense to arrange for the meeting facility and for your accommodations and travel to and from the site. Now, imagine that, after only six hours of meetings, your work team has resolved every outstanding issue brought forward.

What happens next? Do you acknowledge your success and return home early, or do you perhaps take the remaining time to partake of the scenic pleasures and activities that await you outside the meeting room? Chances are, if you are like most of us, you will continue to meet—long after the reasons for meetings have ended.

While this problem is prevalent in any kind of meeting, it is especially noticeable in off-site meetings. Whether it is guilt, or some other reason, we are reticent to end a meeting when someone—our employer, our boss, our club— has gone to some trouble or expense to set it up.

It is critical that we all develop a sense of when we have achieved our objectives and can put our meeting to rest. It's just as important, however, that we also learn to recognize when there is no hope for further progress towards our goals, despite our best efforts, and the best course of action is to end the meeting.

## MEETINGS ARE INEFFICIENT AND UNPRODUCTIVE

It's no secret that many meetings are inefficient and unproductive. We have all experienced more than our share of such meetings. Have you ever been in a meeting that seemed to last forever, but after all was said and done, failed to achieve any meaningful results? Or have you ever been in a meeting that was totally out of control and where discussion careened from topic to topic with no apparent purpose and with no obvious relationship to the subject of the meeting? If you have, you have experienced inefficient and unproductive meetings first-hand.

In this chapter, we name the reasons for inefficiency and unproductive behavior in meetings. We can find these reasons throughout most any organization—regardless of how enlightened or how people-oriented it is. It is the nature of the beast that, unless individuals or organizations make a conscious effort to make meetings more productive, they won't be.

Most of us put up with these ills of meetings as a basic fact of business life. We tend to assume that a certain percentage of meetings, which number varies from person to person, are going to be unproductive and inefficient. In fact, a good meeting often comes as a surprise. Instead of taking an active role in fixing the underlying causes of poor meetings, too many of us just take meetings for granted and live with the results—good or bad.

The real shame is that the costs of inefficient and unproductive meetings, which some would cavalierly write off as just a basic but unfortunate fact of life, are very real. These costs are so real and so high, that they threaten to strangle the lifeblood out of many otherwise vigorous organizations.

Take for example, the following scenario (see Exhibit 2–1). A biotech firm has 100 managers, distributed across several levels within the organization. Although you may personally spend more time in meetings, we will use conservative numbers for our example. The high-level managers spend on average 12 hours a week in meetings. The middle-level managers average 10 hours a week in meetings, and the lower-level managers average 8 hours a week in meetings. For purposes of this example, we will ignore the fact that there are many other people in the company who regularly participate in meetings besides managers.

The firm has a pretax income of $4 million on $50 million of sales. We have assumed a meeting efficiency of 47 percent, as suggested in extensive research conducted by experts in organizational behavior.

In this example, the annual cost of inefficient meetings is nearly $700,000—and this accounts only for the company's managers. If you were to consider the effect of inefficiencies in meetings attended by all employees, it is easy to imagine a total annual cost that approaches $1 million per year for a company with 500 employees. For a company with revenues of $50 million per year, and pretax income of $4 million, the loss of $1 million per year due to ineffective meetings is tragic.

**EXHIBIT 2-1**
*An Example of the High Cost of Meetings*

| Position and Number of Employees | Burdened Labor Rate Per Hour | Number of Hours in Meetings Per Week | Totals |
|---|---|---|---|
| High-level managers (20) | $40 | 12 | $9,600 |
| Mid-level managers (35) | 30 | 10 | 10,500 |
| Lower-level managers (45) | 20 | 8 | 7,200 |
| Weekly cost of meetings | — | — | 27,300 |
| Annual cost of meetings | — | — | 1,310,400 |
| Estimated meeting efficiency (@ 47%) | — | — | 615,888 |
| **Annual cost of ineffective meetings** | — | — | 694,512 |

Exhibit 2-2 describes the hourly cost of meetings to an organization. Take the average of the annual salaries of all participants and find the number of participants in the meeting. This gives you the total hourly cost of the meeting. Now, if you consider that approximately one-half of all meeting time is wasted, you will begin to get some sense of how much money is wasted each and every hour that you meet.

So, as you can see, it is clearly in our interest to make meetings more productive and more efficient. In many cases, the profitability and, ultimately, the ability of our organizations to survive and prosper in these tough economic times, depend on it. We can no longer sit idly by, content with the status quo, as our nation's competitiveness in world markets is slowly but surely eroded away.

**EXHIBIT 2–2**
*Hourly Cost of Meetings*

|  | *Annual Salary* | | | | | |
|---|---|---|---|---|---|---|
|  | *$20,000* | *$30,000* | *$40,000* | *$50,000* | *$60,000* | *$70,000* |
| *Number of Participants* | | | | | | |
| 1 | $10 | $16 | $21 | $26 | $31 | $36 |
| 2 | 21 | 31 | 42 | 52 | 63 | 73 |
| 3 | 31 | 47 | 63 | 78 | 94 | 109 |
| 4 | 42 | 63 | 83 | 104 | 125 | 146 |
| 5 | 52 | 78 | 104 | 130 | 156 | 182 |
| 10 | 104 | 156 | 208 | 260 | 313 | 365 |
| 15 | 156 | 234 | 313 | 391 | 469 | 547 |
| 25 | 260 | 391 | 521 | 651 | 781 | 911 |
| 50 | 521 | 781 | 1,042 | 1,302 | 1,563 | 1,823 |
| 100 | $1,042 | $1,563 | $2,083 | $2,604 | $3,125 | $3,646 |

Note: All figures are based on labor cost only and do not include costs of fringe benefits or overhead.

## LACK OF PREPARATION

If there is one specific reason for most failed meetings, it is surely the failure of the participants to adequately prepare. It is a simple but compelling fact that the amount of preparation the participants involve themselves in directly relates to the ultimate success of the meeting. If you or the other meeting participants have not sufficiently prepared, there is no question that it will be inefficient. The only question is how inefficient it will be.

At a minimum, you should familiarize yourself with the background of the meeting issues. You may not have enough time to do a thorough job, but try to become knowledgeable about the topic. Research it thoroughly. Try to anticipate the points of view of the other meeting participants. Request the input of your staff and co-workers.

While it is certainly not possible to anticipate each and every facet of a topic, good research can turn up tons of information that can be very valuable in a meeting. This information will make your meetings much more efficient and effective. How can you become better prepared? Talk to co-workers who have dealt with this issue before. Review correspondence, reports, and other documentation on the subject. Read company policies and procedures. Network with your customers, suppliers, or other business associates. There is no limit to the number of potential sources of information that you can approach as you prepare for your meeting.

The solution for being unprepared is easy—take the time to get prepared before the meeting starts. If you are totally unprepared for a meeting, consider postponing it until you have a chance to prepare. You'll be doing the other participants, and your organization, a big favor by not wasting their time trying to get up to speed during the course of the meeting. Although there may be considerable time pressures compelling your participation regardless of your level of preparedness, take our word for it—if you adequately prepare for your meeting, you'll discover better, more complete solutions to your problems in a shorter period of time.

## TOO MANY EGOS

Unfortunately, the very thing that makes meetings an especially effective organizational tool can also cause them to fail. It is the element of real-time human interaction that sets meetings apart from other, less interactive forms of business communication. For all the good things that face-to-face human interaction brings, there are also numerous negatives we must overcome for a meeting to be successful.

Some people believe, for example, that an invitation to a meeting is an invitation to dominate the discussion, put down other team members, or refuse to consider the needs of the entire organization over their own parochial interests. If we don't rein in these out-of-control egos, the negative effects on meetings and on the company's employees can be extensive and long lasting. (We will discuss specific techniques for controlling people who try to dominate meetings in a later chapter.)

> There's three things you can predict in life: tax, death, and more meetings.
>
> —Mike Moore

Take, for example, the case of a marketing vice president in a local software development firm. Mark is the Teflon vice president. It seems that, no matter what kind of predicament he gets himself into, he is able to deflect the blame quickly and easily. He sees his job strictly in terms of taking clients out to lunch, jetting around the world while racking up hundreds of thousands of frequent-flier miles, and making promises to potential customers that the company's project managers can rarely keep. Mark has always had a knack for deflecting any real work assignments. This talent is especially evident in meetings.

When the topic of conversation permits, Mark is always a strong advocate of other departments working overtime to get a proposal out to a customer. But, when it comes time for Mark to help out, it seems he always has something else to do.

✴ ✴ ✴ ✴ ✴

"Gotta call Paris! Maybe I can line up Air France for a system demo. Once they see it, they'll have no choice but to buy tons of our product!"

And, when Mark isn't busy deflecting work assignments, he is busy showing off his extensive knowledge of business and putting down everyone else.

"Look, I've been in this business for 20 years. Don't try to tell me about our customers! I have more knowledge about our customers in my little finger than you or anyone else in the organization will ever have. I know what they want. I know what they don't want. You can just take your so-called marketing surveys and toss them in the trash. If it wasn't for me out there holding their hands, you guys wouldn't even have a job!"

✴ ✴ ✴ ✴ ✴

The next time one of these know-it-alls shows up in your meeting, do everyone a favor and tell him you won't be needing his services. We can guarantee that your meeting will run a lot smoother, and you'll get a lot more done in a much shorter period of time.

Other meeting attendees like nothing more than to pontificate about subjects that have little or no relation to the major meeting topics. These people love to hear themselves talk. It's difficult, at best, to make meetings work when they are dominated by people who are more interested in their own personal gain than in the gains of the group as a whole.

Meetings should not be forums for the display of hierarchical dominance or one-upsmanship. Unfortunately, we have all participated in meetings where the primary goal of participants was to assert their own parochial interests rather than to work towards achieving the stated goals of the meeting. Instead of sharing their energy with the group in a positive way, these egomaniacs instead regularly choose to concentrate on themselves, and on their own self-centered needs.

## TOO FEW LIONS

Unfortunately, too many meetings are populated with sheep—people who are far too comfortable with the status quo and who loathe the idea of speaking up or bucking the system. For these people, meetings are a necessary evil—to be tolerated, but certainly not welcomed.

You can probably recall the lions in your high school or college classes. The lions were the people who always volunteered to be called on by the teacher. They sat in the front of the classroom and raised their hands more often, higher, and more confidently than anyone else. They were the ones who were prepared for their assignments and who rose to the challenges that their teachers threw out to the classroom. And, invariably, the lions had a few challenges of their own to feed back to their teachers. Of course, if you asked a teacher who she most enjoyed teaching, she would tell you that the lions were the most demanding students, and the most satisfying to teach.

The sheep, on the other hand, were the students who did everything possible to avoid being called on. They hid in the back of the classroom and kept as low a profile as was humanly possible. If it weren't for an occasional sneeze or cough, you might have forgotten they were there at all. They might have done well on their tests, and even made an "A" but, for all practical purposes, their impact on the learning process of the class was a big "F."

It's a rare meeting where everyone participates equally. There are always those participants who prefer to blend into the background, hoping they will not be noticed. Obviously, people who attend meetings but don't participate are a tremendous waste of time to the system. These people waste your time, the time of the other participants, and the organization's time, as well as their own time.

We need lions in our meetings. We need people who have a passion for the topic under discussion. Lions make things happen. Lions provide forward motion in a meeting. They generate ideas. They stimulate discussion. They push the edges of the envelope.

Sheep, on the other hand, do little more than act as living wallpaper. People who don't contribute to the meeting act as anchors that weigh down the meeting with their presence, while adding nothing.

Your meetings will be much more productive if you take the time during the course of the meeting to try to turn the sheep into lions. And, if not lions, at least something in between. If a person has information or a perspective that is important to the outcome of a meeting, be sure to ask for it!

And, while you're at it, do something with those big egos, too. While the big egos often put on an entertaining show—omniscient and full of fireworks—your meetings will be much more efficient if you can get past the show and get to the heart of what they know.

## YOU GET WHAT YOU REWARD

It's an unfortunate fact that most of us really do not want real opinions from those who work for us. Although we may insist that we want people to speak their minds, the evidence overwhelmingly shows that we prefer those who agree with us over those who disagree with us. It's natural for people to want to be the bringers of good news rather than bad news. It's also just as natural for people to want to encourage group harmony rather than conflict. There are always individual exceptions to these rules, of course, but in general this is the case.

You get what you reward. If you reward people for speaking their minds, they will. If you punish those who speak their minds, they will stop. It's that simple.

Who do you want in your meetings? Do you want people who are unafraid to tell you the truth, or would you rather have people who only tell you what they think you want to hear? We hope that you chose truth over temerity.

If you did decide that the truth is what you want out of your meeting participants, you have to make a point of telling them this and then regularly reminding them of it.

You will have to make a concerted effort to ensure that you're getting the straight scoop from your fellow group members. If you sense that you have yes-men and yes-women in your meeting, directly challenge their assertions and press them to give their honest opinions. Eventually, once the participants see you are serious, you'll find that the truth is not quite so hard to obtain.

## Chapter 3

# Why Meet?

**Objectives:**

- To explore valid reasons for meeting, and valid reasons for not meeting.
- To describe the basic rules of meeting management.
- To show how tools like agendas and goal-setting can help you make your meetings more effective.

Before you attend another meeting, take the time to ask yourself: *Why am I meeting? What are my goals? What will my participation add to the success of my organization?* We firmly believe that much of the fault for the pervasive failure of meetings can be directly attributed to our individual and collective loss of vision in the meeting process. Meetings are not inherently poorly run, it is the people who allow meetings to get off track and lose focus, along with those who blindly follow along, who are primarily responsible for meetings that fail.

There are many, many very good reasons to meet. Properly utilized, meetings can be a very efficient and effective means of making participative decisions and communicating information within complex organizations quickly and widely.

The fact that many meetings are doomed to failure is not a valid reason for abandoning them altogether. Instead, the failure of meetings in an organization should be a wake-up

call to management that valuable resources are being
squandered away, and that decisive and immediate action
should be taken to repair the damage to the organization
and to prevent further damage from occurring. And, as we
have already seen, the very real financial and personal
damage within an organization can be extensive and
severe.

The secret is for us to answer the most basic question of
our participation in the meeting. That is, we all should take
a very close look at why we are meeting in the first place.
Once we have determined *why* we are meeting, we can
focus on the individual elements that will make the meeting as efficient and effective as possible. These elements—
the goals of the meeting, who will attend, when to hold the
meeting, where to hold the meeting, and the content of the
agenda—are all important pieces of the successful meeting
puzzle.

## REASONS TO MEET

So, why meet? In these days of rapid advances in communication and information technology, it would seem that
we should be able to eventually dispense with meetings altogether. What with teleconferencing, electronic mail, and
facsimile machines, we can all stay in constant communication with our co-workers without any personal, face-to-
face contact whatsoever during the business day.

But technology has done little to supplant the need for
meetings. If anything, technology has increased the need,
as we all race to keep up with the increased speed and frequency of information flows.

The answer to the question, *Why meet?* is that we have
no choice. Just as the salmon has no choice but to swim up-
stream each year to spawn, so we have to meet. We have to
meet just to stay afloat in the rocky seas of information and

change that flood our organizations. Meetings provide the psychic life preservers that give us at least some semblance of stability in these rapidly changing times.

Regularly scheduled staff meetings are a prime example. How many times have you patiently (or perhaps not so patiently) sat through a one- or two-hour staff meeting where not one item of discussion pertained to you or to your department? Regularly scheduled meetings can be real time wasters. They tend to sweep up large groups of people for long periods of time—whether or not these people have anything to contribute to the outcome or learn from the discussion. Also, since regularly scheduled meetings are just that, they often are continued to be scheduled even when the original purpose for the meeting has vanished.

A close acquaintance of one of the authors used to work in the material control department of a large aerospace corporation. Every day, without fail, the lead supervisor called a half-hour department meeting to discuss changes in material code numbers. Attendance for the group of 30 employees was mandatory. On the surface, the requirement for all employees to attend this meeting might not seem unreasonable. At least until you realize that in only one or two meetings during the course of the week did the code number changes affect the work that each individual employee performed. The balance of the daily meetings were a complete waste of time for the other employees.

The sad thing is that the same was true for everyone. On any given day, these code changes affected only a small portion of the overall group. On average, at least 70 percent of the time spent by all 30 employees in these regularly scheduled meetings was completely wasted.

Was there a reason to meet? Yes—the material code changes needed to be communicated to the affected employees. Did the meeting serve its purpose? Yes, it did. But was the meeting handled in the most efficient way possi-

ble? No, it wasn't. It would have been much more efficient
to find an alternative way of getting the information to the
affected employees without wasting everybody else's time.
For example, it would be much more efficient for someone
to sort out the code changes by employee and then directly
communicate them by way of memo or perhaps by limit-
ing meeting attendance only to those employees affected
by that particular day's material code changes.

There are plenty of reasons to meet. But just because
there are reasons to meet, doesn't necessarily mean you
should. Especially if you haven't taken the time to define
the critical elements for having a successful meeting that
are further explained in the sections that follow.

## GOALS OF GROUP MEETINGS

Do you have any idea what your goals really are? If not,
you had better take the time to figure them out. How can
you tell what direction to point your meeting if you don't
know where you're going?

The most important task of the budding meeting practitioner, even before determining who to invite, when to
meet, where to meet, or what to meet about, is to determine exactly what your goals are. Depending on what
your goals are, you will determine the participants, when
the meeting will be held, where the meeting will be held,
and what items will be placed on the agenda. If you wait
until you start the meeting to determine your goals, much
of the meeting will be spent trying to define the goals
rather than actually reaching the goals.

If you are the meeting leader, be sure you have defined
the goals of the meeting before you do anything else.
Once you have defined your goals, then draw up your list
of meeting participants and define and publish the
agenda. If you are a meeting participant, and the goals of

the meeting are not made clear to you before the meeting is scheduled to start, press the meeting leader to define them.

## WHO, WHY, AND HOW MANY?

It is rarely intuitively obvious who should be invited to a meeting and who shouldn't be. Sure, staff meetings and the like are no-brainers—you just invite the whole department and you're all set. When, however, you are trying to solve complex problems or make decisions that affect large segments of your organization, or cross interdivisional lines, the decision as to who to invite to your meeting becomes infinitely more complex.

Too many group members make for ineffective meetings. There is a point of diminishing returns in any meeting where, as you add more attendees, you actually decrease the effectiveness of the group. A graph of this function appears in Exhibit 3–1.

Depending on the meeting type, the nature of the organization, and the roles of the participants, productivity increases as each new group member is added. At some point, the number of attendees is ideal for the meeting, and group productivity is optimized. However, as we add additional participants beyond this optimal point, group productivity begins to decline. Meeting leaders must ensure that meeting attendance doesn't get out of hand.

In an article in *Fortune* magazine, Laurel Cutler, director of global marketing and planning for the FCB/Leber Katz ad agency, claimed that the most efficient meetings have only two attendees. In these meetings, the two participants make a decision and agree on a plan for its implementation.[1] This no bells and whistles approach to meeting management boils down the purpose of a meeting to its barest essentials.

**EXHIBIT 3–1**
*Meeting Productivity as a Function of the Number of*
*Participants*

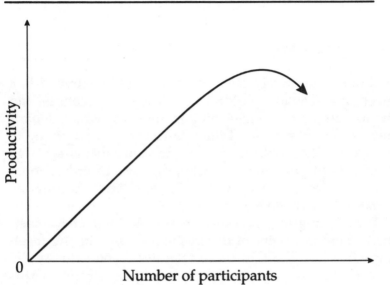

The first rule of thumb is to invite only those members of the organization who are directly affected by or have relevant information on the topic to be discussed. Using this rule of thumb confers two definite benefits. First, you exclude any individuals who, since they aren't directly affected by the outcome, will have only marginal real interest in the meeting process or whether the goals of the meeting are achieved or not. Second, you ensure that at least some of the participants will be close enough to the process to make your meeting much more meaningful and substantive, which makes the probability of your meeting the goals of the meeting much more likely.

A good second rule of thumb is to invite only those people who have a commitment to the topic to be discussed. It's not enough to be affected by the process being discussed. It is also necessary to be excited by the prospect of having their voices heard and actively participating in reaching solutions. There's nothing worse than having to cheerlead a group of people who would much rather spend the meeting time working on their impersonations of dead wood.

The third rule of thumb is to invite the minimum number of participants necessary for you to reach your goals, while obtaining the broadest cross section of opinion possible. It may be that you have an overabundance of meeting candidates available who meet the first two criteria of being directly affected by the issue and having a passion for the issue. In this case, whittle the list of invitees down to a small group that includes a diversity of background, experience, and opinion. By doing this, you ensure that you will obtain the best solutions possible with the minimum number of employees. In other words, your meetings will be both efficient and effective. What more could you ask for?

Before you call a meeting, always take the time up front to determine who should attend, and why. Make a list, then pare it down to the essentials of who is really necessary to get the job done. By taking the time to complete this relatively painless task before you meet, you can ensure that your meetings will always have purpose and will always be as efficient and effective as possible.

While every situation is different, in general, the ideal meeting team size is six to eight participants. As the group of participants gets larger, it is often beneficial to break into subgroups to maintain overall efficiency and productivity.

Don't be afraid to test the limits. The next time you schedule a meeting, draft your usual list of attendees . . . then cut it in half. Keep only those individuals most necessary to the successful outcome of the meeting. If the meeting isn't achieving its goals, you can always add more participants anytime you desire.

Also, don't be too concerned that by excluding members of your organization you will hurt their feelings. Too often we have observed managers who will invite staff members to attend meetings—not because they have an interest in the process, or have anything particular to add—but merely because they want to prove to their employees that management "cares" about their opinions. Standing committees are particularly troublesome. Reconsider their need, and don't be afraid to disband them if warranted.

If a potential invitee is not there to make an active and profound contribution to the meeting, then he or she shouldn't be there at all. Let us say it again: Never let yourself succumb to the charity method of meeting management. In these days of employee empowerment, it is ever so tempting to do so, but don't let it happen to you.

## SCHEDULING

We all know the feeling of having a day that is completely booked with meetings. As soon as you finish one meeting, it's off to another one. If you're lucky, you might get a chance to surface to retrieve your phone messages or shuffle through your in-box at least once or twice during the course of the day. You also are no doubt familiar with the frustrated feeling you get when your carefully orchestrated meeting schedule is thrown into complete disarray when the participants for your first meeting show up half an hour late.

Schedules are a very important element in successful meeting management. To begin, meeting schedules should be rigid enough for the participants to be able to plan around, but malleable enough to allow for some flexibility in reaching a solution if a meeting is going particularly well, but is running overtime.

A committee is something that keeps minutes but
wastes hours.

—Anonymous

If a meeting is scheduled to start at 9:00 in the morning,
then insist that all the participants be ready to start the
meeting at 9:00. It's a waste of time for everyone when the
start of a meeting is held off until everyone shows up. In
some organizations, it is routine for meeting attendees to
routinely show up 10, 15, even 20 minutes late. Some people even use their lateness as a subtle way of proving to
their co-workers how important they are.

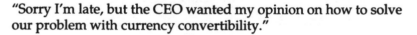

"Sorry I'm late, but the CEO wanted my opinion on how to solve
our problem with currency convertibility."

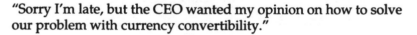

On the flip side of the coin, if you say a meeting is going
to last an hour, then do everything possible to end the
meeting on time. While it may often be tempting to allow
the meeting to run into extra innings, especially if you got
off to a late start or the meeting is going particularly well,
remember that the participants all have their own schedules and commitments they need to honor.

We're not suggesting by any means that you become a
time management freak. It seems that the current fad
among rabid time management adherents is to conclude
all meetings at *exactly* the time originally agreed to—despite the fact that substantial progress is being made at that
moment towards achieving the meeting goals and the participants are all willing to stay until the meeting reaches a
natural conclusion.

These compulsive time managers have little or no re-
gard for the living, breathing quality of meetings. Instead,
they rely on unduly rigid and artificial methods to try to
manage meetings. While a strict, authoritarian approach to
schedules may hold novelty for some, this is not the meeting cure-all that some make it out to be.

Set schedules, but allow plenty of flexibility in your
schedules to accommodate the unanticipated breakthrough, or the unexpected epiphany. We cannot legislate
creativity through strict scheduling and clock watching.
We should, however, make it a habit to respect the schedules and commitments of those we invite to participate in
our meetings. As an aid to accomplishing this goal, consider asking for a member of the group to watch the time.

## SET GROUND RULES FOR ALL
## PARTICIPANTS

In any meeting, it is important to set ground rules. Even
though you might use an agenda in your meeting, an
agenda by itself doesn't do the whole job of telling the
meeting participants what they can expect out of the meeting process. Ground rules provide meeting participants
with firm boundaries within which they can work and a
firm foundation on which to build your discussion.

We can all waste a lot of time feeling our way around if
we don't know where the boundaries of a meeting lie. It's
sort of like playing blind man's bluff. After you've been
blindfolded and then spun around so that you're completely disoriented, you're not going to charge ahead at
full speed looking for the object of your search. Not unless
you're in the market for bruised knees and a lot of close
encounters with immovable objects.

No, if you're like most of us, you will slowly, cautiously
feel your way around the landscape, seeking the bound-

aries, the pitfalls, and obstacles of your environment. Only after you have become comfortable with your new surroundings will you begin to accelerate your search.

To help *everyone* work at peak efficiency, without having to feel their way around an uncertain environment, it is imperative that you make the meeting ground rules clear to all participants at the beginning of the meeting. Once you develop your own consistent meeting style, then it will not be as important to repeat these rules in future meetings with the same group of attendees. After awhile, everyone will get used to your style and internalize your ground rules as a natural baseline of their meeting behavior.

So, what ground rules are the most appropriate for your meetings? Each type of meeting is different, and the ground rules applied to each meeting type will necessarily be different. The ground rules you select will also vary depending on your own personality or management style.

Is your management style dictatorial and rigidly hierarchical? If so, you'll want to let the participants know that, regardless of the outcome of the meeting, you may very well decide to reject the recommendations of the group and pursue your own options. It's a much better idea to let the group know this fact up front rather than build up their expectations and, ultimately, seal their disappointment if you discard the group's recommendations in the process of making your final decision.

Perhaps you're going to hold a brainstorming meeting, and you want to ensure that you obtain the widest variety and the greatest quantity of ideas as an outcome of the process. In that case, before the meeting starts, you should explicitly announce to the group that you want to hear any and all ideas they have to offer—no matter how far out in left field they may be. You should also announce that you will not tolerate the criticism of individuals or ideas by any member of the group since criticism will only serve to curtail the flow of ideas by those group members who are criticized.

There are, of course, many other possible ground rules that you can effectively utilize in your meetings. We have developed the generic set of six rules that follow as an aid to conducting any sort of meeting. A summary of these ground rules can be found in Exhibit 3–2 on page 42.

### Ground Rule #1

**Announce the length of the meeting and promise that the meeting will begin and end on time.** There are few things worse than enduring a meeting that drags on well past the planned time for conclusion. *Especially* if the meeting is going nowhere fast.

You know how good it feels (and how rare it is) to accomplish your goals and complete a meeting ahead of schedule. Not only are you excited by the prospect of salvaging a few precious minutes in your busy schedule, but you feel like you really accomplished something extraordinary.

When a meeting drags on beyond its allotted time, an equal and opposite reaction occurs. Instead of feeling excited by our progress, we grow progressively more and more anxious—wondering when we'll wrap up the meeting and be able to return to our regular tasks or get out of work on time to beat the rush hour. And, instead of feeling we have accomplished something, the longer the meeting goes past the agreed-upon ending time without a successful conclusion, the more we feel that the meeting is in trouble and that we are being personally held captive.

Start your meetings on time and end them on time. If a meeting is going to run overtime but a definite conclusion has not yet been reached, schedule another meeting to deal with the remaining issues. If you do decide, for whatever reason, to allow a meeting to go beyond its allotted time, do so *only* with the express agreement of the participants. If some of them insist on leaving, then don't pressure them to stay—their hearts won't be in the meeting anyway.

### Ground Rule #2

**Distribute the agenda and any prework in advance.** You want your meetings to be as efficient as possible. This means that you want the participants to be prepared to discuss the topics and to make well-considered recommendations. These goals can be accomplished only if all meeting participants have an idea of what will be discussed at the meeting.

We have seen this phenomenon repeated time and time again as the meeting time approaches. When an agenda or other meeting materials or assignments are distributed in advance of the meeting, we know exactly what to prepare for, and we do. Unless we like being caught unprepared, we will make sure that we are familiar enough with the topics to be conversant with them, if not expert in them.

### Ground Rule #3

**Modify the agenda with the group.** Using an agenda helps all participants, including the meeting leader, do a better job of focusing on the primary meeting topics, and it helps the meeting leader keep the meeting discussion on track. It can be very beneficial, however, to get the group's input. Once the meeting starts, discuss the agenda with the group and add or delete items, set priorities, and determine time limits for discussion.

Depending on the input you receive from the group, you may find that some issues have already been solved, and that new ones need your attention. Just because you have typed up your agenda before the meeting doesn't mean it can't be changed. Flexibility, not rigidity, is the key.

### Ground Rule #4

**Be open to new ideas.**   As difficult as it may be to believe, we don't always know everything about every topic that we encounter in our everyday working lives. Yeah, you probably would like to think that you do (we know *we* would), but it's just impossible for any of us to see every angle of every complex problem that comes our way.

Always let the participants in your meetings know that you are receptive to new ideas—*especially* if you're not. Make a point of telling them that you value their input. If you're not open to the ideas of those in your meeting, your body language will telegraph the message to everyone loudly and clearly. And once that particular message is received by the meeting participants, you can guarantee that they will clam up faster than you can say *boo.*

In problem-solving meetings, the reason you have invited other people to attend is to get new perspectives and new ideas for solutions to your problems. If you're going to go through the trouble of calling a meeting, and if you are sincerely looking for solutions, then at least be open to the new ideas that your group offers up for discussion. Who knows—you will probably learn something in the process.

### Ground Rule #5

**Solicit the group's participation.**   Occasionally, participants in meetings feel inhibited from speaking up. The reasons for this can vary widely. Some employees may be afraid to speak their minds in the presence of higher-ups in the chain of command. Some participants may not want to criticize the status quo. Some individuals may be shy and uncertain about speaking in front of their peers. Still others may simply lack an interest in the topic.

It's important that whoever is leading the meeting create a safe environment for all participants. Everyone should know that their participation and comments won't be used against them in any way, that you want and expect honest and frank discussion to take place.

Invite all members of the meeting group to participate actively in the meeting. Let them know that you value their input, and that you can't solve the problem by yourself—you want and need their help.

If, despite publicizing this ground rule to the group, certain participants still refuse to join in the discussion, they should be excused from the meeting. They are wasting time that could certainly be better spent elsewhere.

### Ground Rule #6

**Have a follow-up mechanism.** Most people who have taken the time to participate in a meeting, and who have made honest contributions and recommendations as a part of the process, want to know the impact of their hard work. Make a commitment to the group to provide feedback to them at some point in the future. The best way of doing this is by way of meeting minutes, action plans, milestone schedules, or simply in a memorandum in which you thank individuals for their participation, then go on to describe how the group's recommendations have been used to solve a problem or improve a process in the organization. The primary goals are to summarize meeting outcomes, state the next steps, and to assign responsibilities.

This documentation does not have to be lengthy or unduly elaborate. It merely needs to be clear and concise. We all want to feel we are a valued and necessary part of our organizations. By making contributions in meetings and then seeing those contributions used to improve the organization, we get the satisfaction of being an integral part of a team.

Ground rules help to clarify the role of each meeting participant. In addition to the six generic rules listed above, consider developing others that you can utilize depending on the type of meeting and depending on your own business personality. Just don't go overboard with your rules. It is far better to have a few concise ground rules that help guide the discussion of a meeting without smothering it, than to overburden the participants with so many rules that they end up spending more time concentrating on them than on trying to solve the problem.

**EXHIBIT 3–2**
*Summary: Meeting Ground Rules for All Participants*

| | |
|---|---|
| *Ground rule #1:* | Announce the length of the meeting and promise that the meeting will begin and end on time. |
| *Ground rule #2:* | Distribute the agenda and any prework in advance. |
| *Ground rule #3:* | Modify the agenda with the group. |
| *Ground rule #4:* | Be open to new ideas. |
| *Ground rule #5:* | Solicit the group's participation. |
| *Ground rule #6:* | Have a follow-up mechanism. |

## PREPARING AN AGENDA

Some books make agendas out to be the be-all, end-all of meeting management. The simple fact is, it's not quite that simple. Agendas are very useful for managing certain types of meetings, for example, public hearings where you need to have a clearly organized road map for public discussion and comment, as well as a hard copy record for the sake of posterity. In other cases, such as a brainstorming meeting, where you don't want to prejudice the group's thought process by presenting preconceived notions of the expected outcomes, agendas may not be appropriate at all.

And just because you have an agenda doesn't mean you have the right agenda for the meeting. Far too many of us give low priority to really planning our meetings. If we do an agenda at all, it is likely that we throw something together at the last minute—hoping that we didn't forget anything of substantive import. This is, of course, a recipe for inefficient and ineffective meetings.

To conduct efficient and effective meetings, we simply have to take the time to carefully plan out agendas, just as we have seen that we should carefully determine who will be invited to our meetings.

Meetings without well thought out agendas tend to wander about aimlessly. And, once the conversation begins to wander, it can be very difficult to rein the participants back in. An agenda acts as an automatic place keeper. As discussion begins to drift, it only takes a quick reference to the pertinent agenda item to refocus the meeting.

Another reason for having an agenda is that it serves as a sort of memory for the person running the meeting. We have lost count of the number of times we have conducted meetings, only to realize that, after the meeting ended, we had forgotten to bring up some important topic for discussion. Agendas don't forget. Even if you accidentally skip over an item, someone is sure to point out your error and return your attention to it.

In planning your meeting, make a list of your goals. What route do you want to take to get to your goals? Are there other issues that should be considered as a part of researching your goals? Is the problem too big to solve in just one meeting? The list should not be too detailed—short bullets that summarize the gist of the ideas are sufficient.

When preparing your agenda, take a very close look at the topics to be discussed. We often make the unfortunate mistake of trying to accomplish too much in each one of our meetings. Instead of having a four-hour meeting with your supervisors on a wide variety of topics—each one of which affects certain supervisors, but not others—consider instead whether it wouldn't be much more effective to conduct a few half-hour meetings targeted only to those supervisors who are directly affected by those particular issues.

We tend to believe that bigger meetings are better meetings. We can be easily misled to think that bigger meetings are more efficient simply because we are reaching a wider audience at one time. Big meetings, however, by their nature tend to be extraordinarily inefficient because there will always be a segment of the group that will have no interest in the topics to be discussed. The time that these people spend in meetings is pure, unadulterated waste.

Small meetings, on the other hand, can be much more efficient because we have focused participation only by those individuals with the greatest interest and passion for the issue. Also, small meetings tend to be much faster because we can cut through the cumbersome dynamics of large group interaction and arrive right at the heart of the issue.

Have you ever bitten off more than your group can chew in just one meeting? This mistake is definitely not uncommon. It's easy, when we are considering all the different problems facing us, to try to solve everything all at once. Of course, just as we can't be everywhere at once, we cannot honestly expect to be able to solve every problem that needs to be solved in just one meeting. Depending on the complexity of the issue, it may take a series of meetings to fully address all the facets of the problem, and develop well thought out strategies and solutions.

Don't succumb to the temptation to overload your agenda. Too many meetings are overwhelmed with agenda items. Instead, focus on a few key issues that are at the heart of the problem. If you can conquer the heart of the problem, the details will follow as a matter of course.

The executive team of a large organization is very busy with any number of political crises and organizational dilemmas. It's hard enough for them to set aside the time to get together for an hour or two every week, much less to be able to address all the items on their meeting agendas. Nevertheless, the executive team meeting agenda consistently lists ten or more items for discussion during the course of their two-hour meeting. It's a rare meeting that results in items higher on the list than number five being addressed. Some items languish at the bottom of the agenda for weeks or months without ever being addressed. Eventually, they drop off the agenda when either the problem goes away of its own accord or some transient perturbation in the earth's Van Allen belts deletes the reference from the executive secretary's computer.

Why put items on an agenda if there is no foreseeable possibility that your group will ever be able to address them? In doing so, you only create distractions that prevent participants from fully concentrating on the most important items—the ones at the top of the agenda. Why not structure your agendas so that they fit the amount of time that you have allotted for the meeting—no more—no less? The sample agenda contained in Exhibit 3–3 is an example of a concise, focused business meeting agenda.

## HOW TO HAVE FEWER MEETINGS

We have spent much of this book so far describing ways to make meetings more efficient and more effective. While these goals are primary in importance to us, the best over-

**EXHIBIT 3–3**
*Sample Agenda*

Agenda

Executive Committee

November 14, 1994

(1) Opening Remarks—Mary Tomkins, CEO.

(2) Presentation/Discussion of 3rd Quarter
Financials—Sam Warner, CFO.

(3) Discussion of Current Marketing Efforts—Sara
Washington, VP Marketing.

(4) Future Product Plans—Tom Segal, VP
Development.

(5) General Discussion—All.

all solution is to participate in fewer meetings, and to find
ways to make the meetings that you participate in work
better. Take a minute to answer these questions:

❑ Do you think you spend too much of your time in
meetings?

❑ Do you often wish you had more time to get your
work done?

❑ Are meetings in your organization a waste of time?

❑ Do you wish you didn't have to work so much
overtime?

If you answered *yes* to any of these questions, there's a
good chance you are a victim of the meeting mania that is
sweeping through American business today.

It's kind of funny how we get pulled into meetings that we haven't asked for. Both of the authors have experienced a tough time avoiding meetings with others who are persistent about getting together—even people we don't know, such as salespeople or new vendors. The fact is that we would learn just as much in a fraction of the time, if such potential vendors would simply mail a brochure.

Regardless of the reason, until recently, one of the authors wasted countless hours every week entertaining any number of salespeople representing anything from ballpoint pens to trash collection services. The way he solved the problem with sales meetings was by delegating the task to his assistant. But while he solved *his* meeting problem, he created a brand new meeting problem for his assistant.

We all get dragged into meetings we would rather not attend. In some cases, we may attend because we think that someone from our department should go, or we don't want to hurt someone's feelings by turning down their invitation. Or perhaps just because the topic holds some limited interest or fascination for us.

What do you do when you get a call from a co-worker who would like you to participate in his or her meeting? Do you take the time to find out exactly what the meeting is about and what the expected outcomes are for your attendance? Or, do you simply check your calendar, find an opening, and agree to attend?

As we discussed earlier in this chapter, participation in meetings should be limited only to the minimum number of people, who are close to the process and who have a passion for the issues, necessary to accomplish the task in an efficient and effective manner. Your primary goal should be to get as much work done with as few meetings as possible.

The way to accomplish this goal is to make a conscientious effort to make a real decision on whether you should attend a meeting or not before you blindly make another commitment to do so.

Stop! Right now! Before you schedule your next meeting, take a couple of minutes to determine if your attendance is both the best use of your time and the best use of the group's time. Don't forget that, for the vast majority of the meetings we attend, our attendance is optional. Just because we are invited doesn't mean we have to attend.

What will happen if you don't attend? Will the group fail to have the critical mass necessary to reach its goals? Could your time be better spent elsewhere?

If you determine that the meeting group can survive without you, don't attend the meeting. Be gracious in declining the invitation, but be firm. Surprisingly, you will undoubtedly offend at least one or two individuals when you decline their invitations. There is an unwritten protocol in business that, unless you have another commitment, you should attend any meeting you are invited to. The theory behind the protocol is that whoever is holding the meeting wouldn't have invited you if he or she didn't think your presence was important for the ultimate success of the meeting. Of course, we know this often is not the case. It is rare that an awful lot of thought is put into the list of meeting invitees. Despite this fact, if you decline the invitation, your action may very well be perceived as a snub against the person or group conducting the meeting. Don't let that deter you. Be honest with your co-workers and with yourself.

Meeting mania has some of its roots in the move towards participative management and the employee empowerment movement. Everyone has meetings to address every possible issue in every organization nowadays. Anyone is empowered to call a meeting to address any issue—no matter how trivial or how tangential the issue may be to the successful, day-to-day operation of the organization. And with this power to call meetings comes the power to invite anyone the individual calling the meeting might conceivably want to invite. Whether that works out to two people or twenty people, people who call meetings are rarely questioned—most people simply attend—like zombies in some 50s grade B science fiction movie.

If, after trying to attend meetings only when absolutely necessary, you find that you are still tied up in far too many meetings, it might be time to take drastic action. Try accepting only every other or, perhaps, only every third or fourth meeting invitation and see what happens. If the organization begins to crumble due to your absence then, by all means, try some other approaches. If, however, the organization seems to do just fine without your presence, then make this system a permanent part of your meeting management skills repertoire.

Whatever system you decide to use, from this day forward, make it a habit to closely examine the reason for your attendance in a meeting before you agree to attend. If there isn't some strong and compelling reason to be there, then opt out. It's your choice to attend—you can't blame anyone else for another wasted minute in another meaningless meeting. If you are spending too much time in meetings, *you* have the ability to quickly and easily make a positive difference in your working life.

Take charge of your schedule! Now!

## Chapter 4

# Meeting Management Tools

**Objectives:**

- To relay the basic principles and techniques of meeting management.
- To explain the importance of talk time distribution to the achievement of successful meeting outcomes.
- To describe effective techniques for closing a meeting and obtaining useful feedback from the participants.

If you do nothing else after reading this book, at least make us this one promise: Never attend another meeting without knowing why you're there. And, once you get there, promise that you won't let the meeting lose its focus without at least trying to do something about it.

This is the heart and soul of meeting management—taking an active, responsible role in the meetings you attend. It means not going to unnecessary meetings. It means not attending meetings unprepared. It means making sure that all meeting participants have the opportunity to make meaningful contributions. It means changing group behaviors toward positive, productive ends. Above all, meeting management means becoming a catalyst in the meeting process rather than just going along for the ride. After attending countless meetings that lacked direction and focus, we developed the Power Dynamics method of meeting management.

The good news is that any participant can make a difference. You don't have to be the meeting leader to use Power Dynamics. Anyone can follow the simple techniques set forth in this chapter to make any meeting much more efficient and effective.

## POWER DYNAMICS PLANNING

Why do you plan? For those of you who are managers, you plan because it is one of the five basic functions that you regularly perform as a manager:

❑ Planning.
❑ Organizing.
❑ Staffing.
❑ Directing.
❑ Controlling.

Unfortunately, what may be the most important of these tasks, planning, is probably the task we devote the least amount of time to. When we plan, we aren't organizing, staffing, directing, or controlling. By nature, we all tend to be firefighters, crisis managers, or damage control experts. When we're in that mode (and when *aren't* we?), we have precious little time to devote to planning.

To plan, we have to set time aside from our "normal" work, and make a concerted effort to eliminate all distractions and competing priorities. While this is not a book on time management, the primary focus of the various methods of time management is to free up more time for busy business people to plan. To be effective, we have to plan ahead—if only a week into the future. Yeah, we know. We hate to plan, too. Planning is mundane—it's not nearly as exciting as ferreting out that error in the spreadsheet that's making all the financial reports track in the wrong direction. But, plan you must—like it or not—if you want to be an effective business person.

The Power Dynamics method of meeting management does not allow for planning by default. It does not allow for just "showing up" to be entertained by the group discussion and process—you know, when you let the events make your plans for you rather than the other way around. Don't be at the mercy of the future; planning is the key to mastering it.

> Is the "goal," the "purpose" not often enough a beautifying pretext, a self-deception of vanity after the event that does not want to acknowledge that the ship is following the current into which it has entered accidentally?
>
> —Nietzsche

## WHO HAS A CRITICAL CONTRIBUTION?

One of the focuses of any meeting should be to get all the information and perspectives out. Especially important are the information and perspectives of the person or persons who are closest to the problem or have expertise about the situation.

Talk time is the percentage of time that each individual participant actually talks in the meeting. While talk time varies considerably from meeting to meeting, certain patterns can be expected to develop during the course of a typical meeting.

It has been shown that the meeting leader typically dominates the discussion in the average business meeting. In fact, leaders tend to talk approximately twice as often as the next most talkative member of the meeting group. Not only do meeting leaders talk more often than other meeting participants, but they talk for longer periods of time each time they speak.

On average, meeting leaders have been found to command slightly less than 50 percent of the talk time available in their business meetings. Some individuals contribute little or nothing to the meeting discussion. One of the best indicators of a successful meeting is the equitable sharing of time among all group members. When all members are contributing equally, the probability is highest that no one person is dominating the discussion and that all group participants are being given the opportunity to make contributions to the discussion. It is a sure sign of trouble when the talk time is dominated by one person, whether it is the meeting leader or someone else.

Exhibit 4–1 shows an example of talk time distribution in a typical business meeting:

**EXHIBIT 4–1**
*An Example of Meeting Talk Time Distribution*

| Typical Meeting Talk Time Distribution | |
| --- | --- |
| Meeting leader | 45% |
| Participant A | 20% |
| Participant B | 5% |
| Participant C | 15% |
| Participant D | 15% |

The reasons for this phenomenon are numerous, but the primary factors are these:

❏ The leader may be the most knowledgeable individual regarding the topic being discussed.
❏ The leader usually has the highest status of any member of the group.
❏ The leader is generally responsible for the actual conduct and running of the meeting.

The first factor is where the leader is most knowledgeable about the topic and has the advantage of experience and/or technical knowledge. Most managers got where they are on the basis of their performance in the lower levels of the organization. Many managers started at the bottom, like the rest of us, and worked their way up to the positions of leadership that they currently occupy.

This being the case, most managers are very conversant in the areas they manage. This gives them an inherent and indisputable advantage when it comes to discussion of the topics that concern them. The advantage that meeting leaders enjoy in technical areas can also extend to the area of administrative knowledge. This is because one of the key duties of a manager is to serve as a link between upper management and the rank and file employees.

The second factor is that the status of an individual often has a tremendous impact on the distribution of talk time in a meeting. The higher the status of the participant, the more talk time he or she is likely to garner, without the interruption of submissive, lower-status participants. The higher-status participant also has a much greater ability to jump into the discussion of other individuals than do lower-status participants. This is easily done through the use of verbal or nonverbal signals that flag the other participants to yield the right of way to the higher-status individual.

Status can be a liability in running a truly effective meeting, and it takes the conscious and concerted efforts of the high-status individual to avoid skewing the meeting away from lower-status individuals whose contributions need to be heard. Even so, the evidence clearly shows that most meeting leaders make little or no effort to ensure equal distribution of talk time among all meeting participants. This fact is proof that, for all the talk about participative decision making and employee empowerment, the reins of power are still closely held by those who are in higher-status positions. If high-status individuals are serious about empowering their employees, the first step they should take in meetings is to *talk less, and listen more.*

Finally, the third factor that tends to result in the dominance of talk time by meeting leaders is the certainty that he or she is responsible for the actual running of the meeting. Consequently, it is difficult for meeting leaders not to be more involved in the actual dynamics of the meeting than the other participants are. Meeting leaders, by nature, have to be active and involved, or they wouldn't be meeting leaders.

To offset this natural advantage, the meeting leader should try to minimize the impact of procedural issues on the meeting. By keeping meetings simple and easily understandable by all participants, this goal can be reached with relative ease.

It is the rare group that will be perfect in obtaining a balance while getting out all pertinent facts. Every meeting will be attended by individuals who are more familiar with the issues than the other participants. These individuals will, of course, tend to contribute more than the participants who are not as conversant on the topics being discussed. However, this being the case, we should still aim for an ideal, equal distribution of talk time among all members of the group.

## DRAWING OUT MINORITY OPINION

Not only are the benefits of equitable talk time real, but they can have lasting impact throughout the organization—even beyond the confines of the meeting or its original participants. As we have seen, everyone in an organization wants to be recognized for his or her value and contributions. By ensuring the ability of all participants to *really* participate in meetings, we help to reinforce our employees' feeling of self-worth, and we also help to build their morale and the morale of the organization as a whole.

Never claim as a right what you can ask as a favor.

—Churton Collins

The first key benefit of equitable talk time is that, as the meeting leader speaks less, the other participants can speak more. Many group members are intimidated by higher-ups in the organization. By providing an environment that encourages the contributions of all participants, the enlightened meeting leader will ensure that the widest variety of input will be obtained from all employees—wherever they are located on the organizational chart.

The second key benefit of equitable talk time is that, by delegating responsibility for running a meeting to subordinates, the manager creates valuable opportunities for employees to learn and practice leadership skills. The smart manager provides as many opportunities as possible for his or her employees to grow. The delegation of meeting leadership tasks is an efficient, and relatively painless, way to develop staff skills and talent.

The third key benefit of equitable talk time is that, by encouraging the contributions of staff at meetings, a manager can demonstrate support of the principles of participative management in a meaningful and useful way. When managers are seen as rational, egalitarian, and democratic, the morale of the entire organization will likely improve. If nothing else, the symbolic value of this show of management trust and support of staff is priceless.

## USING POWER DYNAMICS TO CHANGE GROUP BEHAVIOR

Andrew Grove, the CEO of Intel, regards meetings as essential to the successful management of any business. In an article in *Fortune*, Grove suggests that the lack of discipline is what separates unproductive meetings from productive meetings. To make meetings successful, Grove spells out the following recommendations: First, schedule regular weekly meetings with key subordinates. These meetings should be used to discuss routine questions and comments. Next, require that all meeting leaders determine three or four key points that they want to make rather than presenting a lengthy dog and pony show.

As Grove puts it, "And if someone walks into the meeting with 600 transparencies, you have to be strong enough to say, 'Hey, this is BS. Next time bring no more than 10 or 15 and give us some time to discuss what you present.' "[1]

So, how does the practitioner of the Power Dynamics method of meeting management go about changing group behaviors to optimize meeting efficiency and effectiveness? While there are potentially countless different ways of approaching behavioral change in meeting participants, the methods that follow are sure to go a long way in helping you to optimize your meetings. Feel free to add more to the list.

### *Share the Leadership Position*

Regardless of the countless, real-life models to the contrary in our organizations, it is not mandatory that managers lead business meetings. Unless a manager has made a concerted effort to rein in his influence, it is almost guaranteed that his ideas will dominate the discussions. Whether or not the manager is the expert on the topic, his unfettered participation as meeting leader will undoubtedly squelch the contributions of the rest of the group.

To avoid the negative influences on the participation of other group members, and to avoid the destructive influence of groupthink (a phenomenon that will be addressed further in this section), we advise that, whenever possible, managers appoint a subordinate or colleague to lead their meetings. Not only does delegation of meeting tasks have direct and positive benefits to the dynamics of the meeting but, the manager who delegates important tasks such as conducting meetings to subordinates shows that she trusts and values the abilities and judgment of the subordinate. This, of course, can have a profound and lasting morale-boosting effect on the subordinate, as well as other employees in the subordinate's peer group.

Once the manager has turned leadership of a meeting over to a subordinate, he can choose to participate in the meeting in the role of group member, or he can choose to skip the meeting altogether. The answer to the question of which is the preferred role is situational and must be determined on a case-by-case basis.

In some cases, it may be advisable, or even absolutely necessary, for the manager to serve in the meeting as a subject matter expert. As long as her contributions don't dominate and exclude the valid inputs of the rest of the meeting participants, it may be preferable to include the responsible manager in the meeting, if her perspective will make the meeting more efficient and more effective.

If, however, there is no compelling need for the manager's presence at a meeting, then it will clearly benefit group dynamics if the manager does not attend. Even if the manager skips only one out of every four or five meetings, the positive impact on the group will be measurable.

### Structure the Meeting so the Leader Talks Less and Listens More

This is one of the most difficult changes in group behavior to accomplish, whether you are the group leader or a group member. The simple fact is that, if the meeting leader talks less, this automatically makes more time available for other group members to participate. Nature abhors a vacuum. And, for every minute that the group leader is not talking, he should be listening to the other participants as they talk.

As a manager, and a group leader, it is really difficult to just sit back, shut up, and listen. While writing this book, we made a special point of monitoring our performance as meeting leaders. We quickly lost count of the number of times that we unsuccessfully tried to remain silent for more than a few minutes to let others make their contributions to a meeting. We found ourselves biting our tongues on many occasions to keep from jumping into the discussion with our two cents worth of perspective. If you are a manager, try it sometime. We guarantee that you won't last long.

One technique that does seem to work, however, is for the group leader to be the *last* person to speak on a topic. This has the advantage of getting all views heard without bias or slanting to what is perceived as the "right" answer—the one advocated by the leader. In fact, in some modern day groups the leader is in the room, but sits off to the side listening to the group. He or she intervenes only if asked by the group.

If you're not the group leader, the problem of reining in a leader who talks too much and doesn't listen enough is compounded. Not only do you have the problem of a leader who can't control the level of his participation, but you are also faced with trying to deal with him as diplomatically as possible as you work to change the group dynamic.

We all have a lot on our minds. How many times in the last week have you listened to someone, but not heard what she said because your attention was directed elsewhere? The real art of listening is a skill that could use substantial improvement with most of us.

Be an active listener. Instead of making other meeting participants repeat themselves because of your inattention, take a real interest in what they have to say. Reflect their statements back to them to show that you are listening and that you understand exactly what they are talking about. Above all, take the time to listen. You can't listen if you are talking—no matter how hard you might try. The less you talk, the more opportunities you'll have to listen to the other group members, and the better your meetings will work.

## Bring in a Facilitator

A meeting facilitator can be an effective tool for changing group behavior. A facilitator is an individual who takes care of the details of administering a meeting and who helps to guide the participants through the meeting process. The facilitator doesn't act in the role of a meeting participant, but instead acts as a neutral party whose job it is to make a meeting run as efficiently and effectively as possible.

These are some of the specific roles that facilitators can take on:

❑ Mediator.
❑ Timekeeper.

❑ Agenda enforcer.

❑ Group dynamics expert.

❑ Analytical tools expert.

While he doesn't have to be knowledgeable about the subject of the meeting, a good facilitator *does* have to be *very* knowledgeable about the way meetings work and how to effectively guide them so that they reach their goals quickly and easily.

By employing a meeting facilitator, a group can concentrate on the issues and content of the topic, instead of being distracted by the administrative details or drawn into the dead ends of the group's dynamics. A facilitator, acting as a neutral observer, can divorce herself from the power, personality, and political issues that tend to sway the regular members of the group. By maintaining this position of neutrality, the facilitator can gain the trust of the group, and can be very effective in guiding group behavior and performance.

### Refuse to Let Individuals Digress

A personal pet peeve of ours is meeting leaders who either digress from the subject of the meeting or allow other meeting participants to digress. When we attend a meeting, we do so to solve a specific problem or discuss a particular issue. If the issue has been solved, or if solving the issue is not a priority, we want to get back to work.

Unfortunately, some meeting leaders we have known treated meetings as if they were social hours where participants were encouraged to engage in endless prattle about subjects totally unrelated to the topic of the meeting. Other meeting leaders we have known have allowed members to get so far off the topic for so long that no one could seem to remember why we were meeting in the first place.

The most efficient meetings are those targeted specifically to certain topics, and where those targets are followed as closely as possible. If other topics come up during the discussion, and they are important enough to warrant further discussion, then by all means make a note of them. Then, after the meeting has ended, schedule a separate meeting with the participation of the most appropriate people for some date in the future.

To be as efficient and effective as possible, meetings should be sharply focused and finely tuned. Meetings that digress are like puddles of water that slowly spread out—becoming thinner and less defined as they spread—until they inevitably evaporate in the heat of a hot summer's day. A well-run meeting should be as sharply defined as a high-power laser beam.

### Be Prepared

It may seem obvious, but the better prepared the participants are before a meeting starts, the more likely it is that the meeting will achieve its goals quickly and easily. Every minute spent in premeeting preparation will be rewarded many times over in terms of increased meeting efficiency and effectiveness.

Before you do anything else, take the time to decide what your goals are. Once you have figured out your goals, thoroughly research all the issues that will have an impact on successfully reaching them. The last thing you want to do is turn the first half of your meeting into a fact-finding session. Be ready to meet before you meet. Just as three factors primarily determine the basis for real estate value, *location, location, location,* so too do three factors primarily determine the success of a meeting: *preparation, preparation, preparation.*

One way to be sure that the other meeting participants will have a chance to prepare before the meeting is to issue an agenda in advance of the formal meeting time. Generally, the sooner you can get an agenda out to the participants, the better off you will be. One potential problem with distributing an agenda before the meeting is that, like many other memos we send out every day, it's possible that some of the recipients will just ignore it.

---

Never let the other fellow set the agenda.

—James Baker

---

One way to deal with this problem is to put the name of the person most responsible next to each item. Better yet is to include "desired outcome" or "issues to be considered" with each item. By applying subtle pressure in this fashion, you will motivate the members of the group to be more thoroughly prepared when they arrive at the meeting.

### Stamp Out Groupthink

There is one more pitfall that the group should be alert to and avoid at all costs. This pitfall is "groupthink." Webster's *New World Dictionary* defines groupthink as: "the tendency of members of a committee, profession, etc. to conform to those opinions or feelings prevailing in their group." Because members of the group get along, and the proceedings seem at least on the surface to be brilliantly efficient, groupthink can easily occur without anyone noticing, and all the decisions that the group reaches may be poorly made, regardless of the talent of the individual members of the group.

In a meeting, groupthink is like quicksand. On the surface, everything appears to be normal. However, just as a hiker can stumble into a pit of quicksand with no warning, so too can the members of a meeting group stumble into the pitfall of groupthink.

You may be thinking to yourself: So, what's so bad about groupthink? Sure, a meeting that is in the throes of groupthink will be a pleasant affair, what with everyone being so agreeable and all. However, if you take a close look at some of the more famous blunders caused, at least in part, by groupthink, I think you'll understand exactly what the problem is.

The total lack of defensive preparedness in the Japanese attack on Pearl Harbor on December 7, 1941, which led to our participation in World War II, was at least partly the result of groupthink, as was the Bay of Pigs fiasco in 1961. In more recent examples, the decision to replace the original version of Coke with a new, sweeter Pepsi-like version in the early 1980s was a result of groupthink, as was the space shuttle *Challenger* disaster of 1986. Coke's tremendous marketing blunder revealed a key strategic vulnerability within the Coca-Cola Corporation that, at least up until that point, could do no wrong. It was only after the very loud, and very vigorous, protests of lovers of the old formula were publicized widely by the media that Coca-Cola decided to bring back a relabeled version, called Coca-Cola Classic. The *Challenger*, which exploded shortly after takeoff, killing its crew of seven, was launched despite warnings by NASA engineers that the solid booster rocket o-rings might fail under certain conditions. With millions of dollars at stake for each day of delay in the shuttle launch, NASA officials—in a classic model of groupthink behavior—ignored these warnings and decided to launch anyway.

It is precisely due to the pleasant and positive attitudes that individuals in a group have towards each other that the groupthink phenomenon can take root and prosper, and the critical thinking ability of group members can be destroyed. The primary characteristics of meetings in which groupthink is occurring are the utter and complete lack of conflict. As a result, the group will find that consensus is easy to achieve—*too* easy. Since no one is willing to rock the boat and risk upsetting all that good feeling around the table, the group will tend to make low-quality decisions.

Groupthink is not a conscious event. It is an unconscious group phenomenon that occurs unbeknownst to the meeting participants. Strong group cohesiveness, an overall standard of agreement, differences in member status and rank, and subtle pressures within the group driving member conformance, are factors that foster the occurrence of groupthink. When your group experiences the following symptoms, beware of groupthink—it can't be far away:

❑ Rationalizing away problems. ("It's just a temporary downturn in the commercial real estate market. It's going to bounce back real soon!")

❑ A feeling of group invulnerability. ("We have a greased chute! This product has to be successful!")

❑ The active suppression of any signs of conflict. ("Come on, guys, let's all get on the bandwagon. We can't show any signs of weakness to our competitors.")

❑ The negative stereotyping of potential critics of the decision. ("Aw, those folks are just a bunch of naysayers. We'll show them what it takes to be successful in this town!")

Fortunately, there are several cures to the groupthink phenomenon. One very effective cure is to be sure to invite the participation of one or more devil's advocates—individuals who aren't afraid to frame and present a point of view that is at odds with the prevailing norm in a meeting. An effective devil's advocate will break through the brain fog that has enveloped a meeting and focus discussion on alternative points of view that should be considered by the group. It is important for the vitality and long-term growth of an organization that healthy, constructive dissent be encouraged. It is important for the emperor to be told that his new clothes are not all they are cracked up to be.

Another technique is to consider appointing someone besides the highest status individual to be in charge of leading the meeting. When the high status individual runs the meeting, the other participants naturally tend to defer to him or her. This can sometimes lead to groupthink. If someone else is appointed to run the meeting, then the group won't feel the strong need to pattern all its responses after the desires of the high status individual. This is especially true if the high status individual opts out of the meeting altogether, thus allowing for free and unfettered communication by the members of the group.

Finally, consider alternate ways of gathering information for the meeting. It may be, for example, that when employees are asked to point out problems they are having with their supervisors, they are required to sign their names. A requirement like this will tend to skew the data since it takes an especially brave employee to criticize the status quo and sign his or her name to the criticism. By allowing survey responses to be anonymous, the meeting group may find they will obtain dramatically different feedback from surveyed employees. Exhibit 4–2 provides a summary of the key Power Dynamics techniques discussed above.

**EXHIBIT 4–2**
*Summary of Power Dynamics Techniques*

---

❑ Share the leadership position.
❑ Structure the meeting so the leader talks less and listens more.
❑ Bring in a facilitator.
❑ Refuse to let individuals digress.
❑ Be prepared.
❑ Stamp out Groupthink.

---

# WHEN AND HOW TO CONCLUDE

Just as it is critical that the practitioner of Power Dynamics take constant, concerted, and positive action to keep a meeting on track and performing at peak efficiency, the meeting leader has to know when it is time to bring a meeting to an end. Do you remember the basic axiom of meeting completion that we mentioned earlier in the book? Here it is again.

> End the meeting the moment the objectives are achieved or when progress towards meeting them ceases.

Be alert to the signs that a meeting has reached the end of its productive life. If the meeting has been successful, it will be easy to see the light at the end of the tunnel as a natural conclusion is reached. It is important that you take an active part in ending the meeting then and there, before other participants are tempted to continue discussions on peripheral topics. If people want to stick around and shoot the breeze after the meeting, that's up to them. Just don't let those few hangers-on hold everyone else hostage as they discuss topics of interest only to themselves.

It's even more important to take action to end a meeting when its forward progress has slowed to the point where the cost to benefit ratio of the meeting has swung dramatically away from the benefit side and toward the cost side. Since the determination of cost versus benefit is a very subjective one, the meeting leader has to be especially alert for the signs that a meeting has outlived its usefulness. These are some of the signs:

❑ Lack of definite conclusions regarding an issue as the meeting nears its scheduled ending time.

❑ Dwelling on one agenda item to the exclusion of the rest of the agenda.

❑ Irritability and impatience on the part of the group members.

❑ Meeting participants leaving the meeting early.

❑ People start to look at their watches or get drowsy.

This is where having a facilitator can be especially beneficial. The meeting leader and participants may be wrapped up in emotional or organizational issues that cloud their ability to see that progress has come to a halt or that the group is actually regressing. Sometimes it takes an outsider to see what is really happening within a group.

So, now that you have decided to conclude a meeting, how do you do it? The best way is to summarize the agreements that were reached, briefly review the issues that remain unresolved, and confirm future actions and who is responsible for each. If there is a need to schedule another meeting to wrap up loose ends, take the opportunity to do so while you still have the group together.

Finally, do not, we repeat, *absolutely do not* continue a meeting just because it was scheduled to end at a certain time. While you may have planned for a four-hour meeting, you may find that, after only one hour, your work is complete. If that is the case, then end your meeting and enjoy the eternal and undying gratitude of your co-workers. Take our word for it, no one ever complained that a meeting ended too soon, but we have *all* complained about meetings that outlasted their welcome.

## FEEDBACK MECHANISMS AND EVALUATION

The proper use of the Power Dynamics method requires the active and constant actions on the part of the meeting leader to ensure that every possible means of making a meeting more efficient and effective is explored, pursued, and applied. So, how do you know whether your efforts have truly been effective? How can you determine if there are other possible ways to make your meeting even more effective in the future?

Evaluating your meeting performance and obtaining the feedback of meeting participants is the final step in the complete meeting process, and it is an integral and important part of the Power Dynamics method of meeting management. Evaluation and feedback completes the loop, and can provide valuable insight into the real value of a meeting and supply ideas for improving future meetings.

Meeting feedback can take many forms, but the one most often used is a brief questionnaire that meeting participants are encouraged to complete before they leave the meeting. In Exhibit 4–3, we present one such example. While this format may be suitable in certain situations, particularly for training meetings or other instructionally

**EXHIBIT 4-3**
*Sample Feedback Survey*

---

Meeting Questionnaire

Finance and Accounting Staff Meeting

March 1995


1. Did we discuss all necessary information? If not, what other topics should have been discussed?

2. What did you like about the meeting?

3. What did you not like about the meeting?

4. Were you satisfied with the pace of the meeting?

5. Do you have any suggestions that would make future meetings better?

---

based formats, written questionnaires are generally far too cumbersome for most routine, everyday business meetings.

Realistically, the best way to get feedback from meeting participants at the conclusion of most meetings is to do so verbally—as succinctly as possible. We're all busy, but none of us is too busy to spend a minute or two discussing the benefits of our meetings and ways to make future meetings even better. In eliciting the feedback from meeting participants, you should consider the following factors:

❑ Were all critical topics discussed? If not, what topics should have been added? Which topics should have been deleted?

❑ Was the composition of the group the most appropriate one for the meeting? Would the meeting outcomes have been better if certain people had attended who did not? Would the meeting have run better if certain attendees had not been invited?

❑ Were there improvements that could be made to the process of the meeting, i.e., did everyone get heard, were interruptions kept to a minimum, did discussions get too heated or emotional?

❑ Are all the issues now resolved, or is there a need for further meetings at some future date? If so, who, what, when, and where?

Now that you have the information, you have to do something with it. To make the Power Dynamics system work for you, *you* have to work with it. Don't just let this valuable feedback languish in your notebook or in a file folder lost in the back of your desk; use the information to make your meetings better! Even if you change only one or two things about your next meeting, every effort you make towards improving future meetings will be time well spent.

## Chapter 5

# Meeting Leadership

**Objectives:**

- To describe the necessary transition from high-directive to high-participative meeting leadership.
- To describe the changing roles of meeting leaders and to explore some of the myths of meeting leadership.
- To demonstrate techniques that will help meeting leaders control their meetings without stifling them.

One of the toughest tasks, especially for those of us from the old fashioned, hierarchical school of business management, is making the transition from authoritative leadership to participative, supportive coaching of our staff and co-workers. As we saw in our discussions of talk time distribution, it can be especially difficult for those of us whose jobs depend on our ability to dominate and direct others through sheer willpower, determination, and force of personality, to just shut up and listen—if only for a moment.

As difficult as it may be for us to learn to coach our employees instead of constantly directing them, it is critical for the long-term success of our meetings that we do so. We all have different perspectives and perceptions of what leadership is and what we expect from our leaders. Some of us want and need strong, directive leadership. Others of us feel stifled by a strong hand at the helm; we want and demand a voice in the management process.

Since meetings are one of the few officially sanctioned opportunities we have to meet with our co-workers and discuss issues of importance to the organization, we have a great opportunity to make real and lasting improvements in our systems of communication and in the morale of our employees. The most effective managers have learned how to effectively manage meetings and refuse to let meetings manage their lives. A sure sign of an ineffective manager is one who has not mastered the skills necessary to manage the complex set of personalities and issues that come to the fore during the course of a meeting.

## WHAT IS GROUP LEADERSHIP?

Above all, group leadership is situational. Depending on the type of meeting and the nature of the tasks to be addressed, group leaders will adopt different styles of leadership. One meeting made up of a certain group of employees may require a highly directive, authoritarian leadership style. Another meeting, held for a different purpose, with a different group of employees in attendance, may require a very egalitarian, participative decision-making leadership style.

The particular leadership style to be employed in a meeting depends on many factors, including the topics to be addressed, the reasons for the meeting, who is leading the meeting, and who is participating, the time to be spent in the meeting, and the overall needs of the organization. Despite rumors to the contrary, there is no evidence that one particular style of meeting leadership is the best for all meeting situations.

The first two questions we should ask are: What kind of meeting is this and what kind of leadership style will help me achieve my goals in the minimum amount of time? The answers to this question should be used to frame a model for meeting leadership. In some cases, such as in brainstorming meetings, we may want to avoid being directive or authoritarian. To do so will only stifle the creativity of the group and result in suboptimal outcomes. The most appropriate leadership model in brainstorming meetings is one that supports group members in their exploration of possible solutions, providing just enough direction to help guide the general bearing of the discussion without preempting the honest and unadulterated input of the group members.

While the meeting leader is probably not intending to make any decisions during the course of a brainstorming meeting, she or he does want enough good ideas to form the basis of an effective decision-making process at some later time. In a meeting of this type, decision making is not an issue. This may not be true, however, in different kinds of meeting situations.

Take, for example, a meeting called to decide whether to close a distant sales office. Each of the meeting participants will likely feel that his opinion is important and that the meeting leader should take his contributions seriously when making a final decision. A meeting of this type requires a mix of participative and directive leadership styles. The first part of the meeting will, of necessity, be highly participative, with the meeting leader seeking out the opinions of her trusted advisors. While many different options, alternatives, and scenarios may be presented, defended, and argued by the participants, at some point the leader will change gears—shifting from a participative meeting style to a directive one—as she enters into the decision-making phase of the meeting.

Most managers believe in consensual decision making—to a point. That point is usually located just to the left of the actual decision. Regardless of the meeting style you select for your meeting, make sure it is clear to all participants before the meeting starts. It can a devastating blow to morale when the group believes that consensual decision making will be the rule of the day but, instead, the meeting leader intends to reserve the decision-making for him- or herself.

## MYTHS OF LEADERSHIP

Although managers may not need their subordinates to make their decisions for them, they *do* need their subordinates' advice and recommendations to make better, informed decisions. Anyone can make a decision. Not just anyone, however, can make decisions that are consistently good. If we can make good decisions just 50 percent of the time, we are probably doing much better than average. The best decisions are not the result of a single person pouring through pages and pages of reports or crunching megabytes of spreadsheets on his computer. The best decisions are the result of a leadership process that pulls together the expertise of the best and the brightest individuals in our organizations, and does so in a way that efficiently and effectively organizes the information so that it can be easily digested by the decision maker.

The evolution of leadership in modern organizations has spun off its own set of beliefs and its own mythology. Some of these beliefs are true, many of them are specious, at best. Let's explore some of the more prevalent myths regarding leadership. Do you recognize any of them in your organization? For your convenience, these leadership myths are summarized in Exhibit 5–1 on page 79.

## The Toleration of Dissent Is a Sign of Weakness

We have all been in meetings where some or all of the participants voiced views that were in direct conflict with those expressed by the leader of the meeting. Sometimes, this dissent can be subtle and rather innocuous. Sometimes, a meeting can explode into shouting matches with an intensity unrivaled by any other event in the organization.

Since dissent is often viewed as somehow disloyal and as a force that works against the development of teamwork in an organization, many managers are uncomfortable with its expression in a group meeting situation. This is unfortunate because the primary goal of a meeting leader should be to get the best information possible—whether or not that information happens to be politically acceptable within the organization at that particular time.

As long as the reason behind the dissent is not malicious or the result of rampant negativism, dissent can be a positive and constructive force in an organization. The fact is, however, that most managers are afraid of dissent, don't handle it well and, as a result, isolate themselves in a sea of yes-men and yes-women. This, of course, leads to groupthink and, ultimately, poor decision making.

In his 1974 book, *Management: Tasks, Responsibilities, Practices*, Peter Drucker cited three reasons supporting the need for dissent in an organization:

❑ Disagreement is needed to stimulate the imagination, to develop the creative solution, and to get away from the fallacy of one right decision.

❑ Disagreement safeguards the decision maker from becoming a prisoner of the organization.

❑ Disagreement alone can provide alternatives to a decision.[1]

Clearly, dissent should be encouraged by leaders, not squelched. Instead of viewing dissent as some sort of organizational weakness, or the toleration of dissent as some sort of personal, managerial weakness, we should view dissent for what it is—a healthy, normal part of the optimal decision-making process.

### The Group Leader Must Be the Most Knowledgeable Individual in the Meeting

It is impossible for any one person to know it all—no matter how much he might try, or how much he might like to think he knows it all. Why do we have meetings in the first place? The reason we have meetings is to gain the collective insight and experience of our employees. There aren't very many managers around with much more than 30 or 35 years of experience in business. By pooling the collective consciousness of our employees, however, we can easily tap into a wellspring of wisdom that can reflect hundreds of years of experience.

Making matters worse is the generally held belief that, not only must the meeting leader be the most knowledgeable individual in attendance, but he should also make a point of demonstrating his informational superiority early and often during the course of the meeting. Not only does this attitude make a meeting leader look like a condescending and patronizing elitist, but the active cultivation of this attitude by meeting leaders is a sure way to shut down the flow of communication from other meeting participants.

An organization is like a huge, four-dimensional jigsaw puzzle in which each of us is but a piece. It takes the contributions of each one of us to make the organization a complete and functioning whole. The leader who does not recognize this fact is doomed to failure and, ultimately, to extinction.

## Meeting Leaders Should Not Share the Leadership Role

Most leaders are afraid to let go of the reins of control and power. We all talk a good story about empowering our employees, and about the importance of the input of our coworkers. The problem is that, when we find ourselves in a group meeting situation—especially as the flames of crisis are nipping at our heels—we tend to forget about all those niceties and quickly return to the one thing that got most of us where we're at in the first place—the ability to exert control and influence over our fellow employees.

It is difficult, at best, for a meeting leader to completely fulfill all the needs of a group in a meeting situation. Despite this fact, many of us try to do it all anyway.

Good leaders recognize the fact that the best leadership is shared by all of the participants in a meeting—one after another—until the meeting is brought to a successful conclusion. In a properly functioning meeting, leadership jumps from participant to participant. One participant may, for example, spell out a new idea for consideration by the group. Another participant might take that basic idea and lay out several scenarios of what might result if the idea is implemented. Still another participant might summarize the progress made by the group, and then proceed to shoot down the original idea and suggest one of her own.

To think that only one individual should conduct each one of these group functions, to the exclusion of the other participants, is shortsighted at best. If this were the case, then why have a meeting? The meeting leader should concentrate the bulk of his activities around the mechanics of making the meeting work efficiently and effectively. The smart group leader will leave the actual content of the meeting discussions to the individual members of the meeting team and to the group as a whole.

**EXHIBIT 5–1**
*Leadership Myths*

---

❑ The toleration of dissent is a sign of weakness.
❑ The group leader must be the most knowledgeable individual in the meeting.
❑ Meeting leaders should not share the leadership role.

---

## KEY LEADERSHIP SKILLS

Every meeting leader has a clear and compelling responsibility to make sure that every possible attempt is made to promote the successful outcome of the meeting. The following steps, summarized on page 83 in Exhibit 5–2, should be taken by meeting leaders in their efforts to make their meetings more efficient and more effective.

### Constantly Seek Clarity

As the meeting leader, it is your responsibility to ensure that all issues are clearly expressed, and that all discussion is fully understood by the meeting participants. Have you ever taken part in a meeting where the discussion turned to a topic that you had little or no expertise in? As the discussion progressed, the jargon and acronyms began to fly faster and more furiously. The only problem was that you had no idea what the heck the rest of the group was talking about. And, due to your desire not to look foolish or uninformed in the eyes of the other group members, you didn't ask for an explanation.

In formal meeting procedures such as is advocated by *Robert's Rules of Order*, a motion for a "point of information" to gain clarity in what is being said takes precedence over all other motions. You cannot move forward without clarity! If someone makes a point, and the point is vague or otherwise unclear, require the participant to clarify the statement before discussion continues. Otherwise, each participant may have his or her own, personal interpretation of the statement and, if you have 10 attendees in the meeting, you will have 10 distinctly different perceptions of what the speaker intended.

A meeting leader needs to be sensitive to the fact that not everyone is going to understand all the intimate details about whatever it is that is being discussed. If an esoteric concept is being discussed or if acronyms are being thrown around like so many hot potatoes, take the time to briefly explain to the group what it is you are talking about. Unless you are *absolutely* certain that the group is knowledgeable about the topic, you shouldn't ask the group if they understand the concepts. In many cases, group members are afraid to show their ignorance in front of their peers. Simply take a moment to explain, and do both yourself and the other members of your group a favor.

### Enforce the Agenda

As we have already discussed, agendas can be very effective tools for making meetings as effective as possible. It isn't enough, however, to have an agenda. For an agenda to have any value in the group meeting process, it has to be closely adhered to by all participants.

It is the job of the meeting leader to ensure that meeting discussions remain sharply focused on the topic or topics at hand. The easiest and most effective way for a leader to perform this task is through the use of an agenda. The agenda provides a very clear and understandable road map for group discussion.

Admittedly, it can be a difficult assignment to strictly enforce an agenda—especially when the group finds itself on a fruitful, but ultimately tangential line of discussion. In this case, regardless of *how* promising and exciting the discussion is, note the basic thoughts and then move back to your agenda. After the meeting is over, you can and should schedule a separate meeting to address the new topics.

Enforcing the agenda also means that any attempts by meeting participants to embarrass each other or to use the meeting as a forum to promote their own parochial interests instead of the interests of the entire organization should be quickly and unceremoniously cut off at the knees. The outbreak of conflict of this sort in a meeting, and the resultant irrational and uncontrolled outbursts that the conflict engenders, will quickly destroy the productivity of the group.

Be acutely aware of the difference between a *constructive*, albeit heated presentation or defense of one's position, and a *destructive*, personal attack on the other participants or the organization. As always, be supportive of constructive efforts to find solutions, and aggressively squelch destructive conflict as soon as it rears its ugly head.

### *Actively Promote Dissent*

Yes, we know. It might seem like we're going out on a limb on this one, but that's not the case. When we say that the meeting leader should promote dissent, we are not suggesting that he or she sanction or tolerate group discord or chaos. Quite the opposite. We are instead suggesting that the smart meeting leader will make it safe to constructively express opinions that run counter to the prevailing conventional wisdom, in an environment that rewards the expression of those opinions instead of punishing it.

We are acquainted with an organization that has traditionally had a *big* problem with this particular point. The person in charge of this organization comes from a very authoritarian and hierarchical background when it comes to the decision-making and meeting process. In at least 95 percent of the meetings that he leads, his role is reduced to making "sell" or "tell" presentations. By sell or tell, we mean that if the ideas of the group are solicited, they are only done so in a transparent attempt to placate his subordinates. Instead, he ends up selling his nonparticipative decisions to the group or, failing that, he turns the presentation into a "take it or leave it" tell. The group members already know that to voice a contrary opinion is to invite the very real possibility of being vigorously chewed out in the presence of the other group members.

In an environment that punishes the expression of alternative points of view, such as the organization cited above, it doesn't take long for employees to learn on which side their bread is buttered. The result is that new ideas, instead of being encouraged, are choked off, and the organization is doomed to fall behind its competitors who have already figured out that it is in their best interest to reward their employees for being innovative and for voicing new ideas and opinions that run counter to the status quo.

### Get the Most Out of Your Team

The meeting leader should limit his or her discussion as much as possible to let the other participants have a chance to make meaningful contributions to the meeting process. While the meeting leader's opinions are surely valuable, too, it is important that they not be allowed to dominate the discussion. The best meeting leaders are those who act as coaches—getting the best possible performance out of the *entire* team. The best meeting leaders also act as referees—ensuring that, in the complex milieu of a typical meeting, the rules of engagement are well defined and closely adhered to, and that those who blatantly and repeatedly disregard the rules are quickly penalized.

During the course of the meeting, the meeting leader should concentrate on the dynamics of the group, and on seeking out ways to fine tune those dynamics until an optimal mix is found. If the meeting leader is too busy talking or is distracted by other, competing priorities, then the efficiency and effectiveness of the meeting will never achieve its highest possible level.

**EXHIBIT 5–2**
*Key Leadership Skills*

---

- ❑ Constantly seek clarity.
- ❑ Enforce the agenda.
- ❑ Actively promote dissent.
- ❑ Get the most out of your team.

---

## HOW TO ENCOURAGE INPUT

We hope that by now you agree that employee input is something that should be encouraged, not discouraged. This is, after all, one of the reasons we sponsor meetings to begin with. Even in the most directive meeting situations, we still want to encourage the input of our employees. For example, let's say that the company's president and chief executive officer has called a meeting to announce some dramatic changes in the organizational structure. He slowly rises to speak.

✱ ✱ ✱ ✱ ✱

"After much deliberation, and after consulting with managers throughout the corporation, we have decided that it is now time to make some major changes in the way we do business."

Although the CEO has spoken often to his subordinates about the importance of communication and the need to drive fear out of the organization, there are few employees—especially within the executive ranks—who did not quake when they were called into the president's office.

"As you know, it has become more and more difficult for us to maintain our earnings during this economic downturn. Revenues are down, costs are up. We know it is time to take drastic action."

No one had escaped the wrath of Khan, the angry chief executive officer. One minute he could be as calm as the first breath of spring on a sunny March afternoon; the next minute he could go off like a wayward tactical nuclear device. His tirades were fabled, and the stories of employees who were publicly upbraided, embarrassed, demoted, fired, or worse, were the stuff of legend.

"Okay, Bob, why don't you turn on the view graph machine?"

As the projector clicks on, it is difficult not to notice that the view graph is upside down. Regardless of this glaring fact, none of the assembled employees is willing to put themselves on the line to point this out, lest they become the next target of the CEO's rage. So, for the first five minutes of the presentation, the view graph remains as it is—upside down—for all to see.

**✳ ✳ ✳ ✳ ✳**

The point is that we should always encourage the input of our co-workers regardless of what kind of meeting we are conducting. Sure, we may expect more input in highly participative meeting environments and less input in highly directive meeting environments, but even the most directive meeting leader should expect and encourage the input of other group members—if only to tell him that the zipper in his pants is unzipped or, heaven forbid, that his view graph is upside down.

The best way to encourage the input of the participants in your meeting is to thank and acknowledge them for their contributions. The quickest way to discourage your co-workers' input is to punish them for providing it. While this may seem trite and obvious, think about the meetings that you personally attend. How often does a meeting leader really seem to want the contributions of the other participants, and how often does the meeting leader merely tolerate or even actively discourage them?

Take a close look at how others in your organization conduct their meetings. Make mental notes of what techniques seem to work for them, and which don't. Then, take the best techniques and try them for yourself. Just keep in mind that it is really quite simple to encourage the input of your co-workers. All you have to do is let them know that you want it—you'll get plenty.

## WAYS TO CONTROL DISCUSSION

While it is not always possible or desirable for a meeting leader to control every single aspect of the natural course of a meeting, there *are* certain avoidable behavioral situations that can significantly decrease the efficiency and effectiveness of a meeting. While the occasional appearance of these behaviors is to be expected, and will not notably affect meeting productivity, the rampant, unchecked expression of the behaviors that follow can quickly and dramatically decrease meeting efficiency and effectiveness.

### Interruptions

Nothing can halt the forward progress of a meeting more quickly than when one or more meeting participants constantly break into the discussion to present views that are tangential and have little or no bearing on the overall

direction of the meeting. While you should always expect a nominal amount of interruptions to the flow of
communication, when those interruptions get out of
hand, the fabric of the meeting quickly unravels with
threads of half-completed trains of thought lying all
about. Once this happens, it takes a particularly concerted effort on the part of the meeting leader to get the
meeting back on course.

Interruptions by meeting participants can ride a very
fine line between the need and desire of meeting leaders to
encourage free and open discussion related to the topic,
and the equally important need to ensure that the discussion remains focused on the agenda items. On the one
hand, you don't want to be too rigid or have too many
rules, as this will only tend to constrain the creative
process of the meeting participants. On the other hand,
you don't want chaos to reign since that, too, will only lead
to decreased meeting productivity.

So, how can you determine when breaking in is good for
a meeting's progress and when it is bad? To get a sense of
this, first ask yourself the following questions:

❑ Are the interruptions detracting from the overall flow
   of communication in the meeting?
❑ Is the person breaking in doing so to demonstrate his
   or her "superior" knowledge or to dominate the
   meeting discussion?
❑ Are the contributions of other participants being
   overridden by the interruptions?

If you answered yes to any of these questions, you have a
situation that requires your immediate attention. Uncontrolled breaking in by group members can only make your
meeting less efficient. And as the interruptions continue
without intercession on your part, the other group members will start to withdraw—leaving you with a meeting
dominated by a small portion of the group.

## *Jumping to Conclusions*

Most of us pride ourselves on our ability to solve problems. For many of us, this has been the key to our success—the ability to quickly and effectively recognize the problem, define it, and then devise and implement rapid fixes or solutions. While this skill may be useful when there is some urgent or compelling crisis to be dealt with, in nonurgent situations, a more relaxed and more thorough and thoughtful review and discussion of the problem would lead to better long-term solutions. Who ever heard of a good physician guessing at a cure without first obtaining an adequate diagnosis of the problem? Yet, in business, there is often a pressure to gain a solution fast, even if it is not the best solution.

Perhaps we are all conditioned to some degree by TV game shows such as Jeopardy and Family Feud where one or two thousandths of a second can mean the difference between success and riches beyond our wildest dreams and interminable defeat, public ridicule, and embarrassment. These games reward those participants who can demonstrate snap judgment and quick reflexes. In business, we tend to do the same thing. We reward those people who can make quick decisions. Not necessarily good decisions, but quick ones.

How many times have you heard the saying that it is better to make a bad decision than to make no decision at all? Of course, the veracity of this statement depends on how bad the decision is. If the decision means that your company ends up in bankruptcy, perhaps it would have been better not to have made a decision after all.

Too often, we find ourselves jumping to conclusions. Instead of taking the time to suspend our judgment while we thoroughly analyze a problem and to carefully consider different options and alternatives, we try to find the quick fix or the instant solution. The desire to jump to conclusions can, at times, be overwhelming.

As a meeting leader, the best way to guard against this phenomenon is to follow a deliberate, methodical route to the solution and to cut off any short circuits that happen to arise during the course of the meeting. Before you go on to the next topic, summarize the one you have just finished. Be sure that the other members of the group are a part of the summary and understand and support it. Otherwise, you are sure to have to backtrack and cover ground that you thought you had left behind long ago.

### Beating Around the Bush

In organizations where there is an environment fraught with fear and employees are routinely punished for speaking up, the result is people who beat around the bush. Instead of pointing out a specific problem that occurs in a specific part of the organization because of the mistakes of a specific system or individual, the bush beater will instead make a generalized statement about a vague problem that may or may not really be occurring at any given time depending on who you ask. And although this problem is causing half of the production of semiconductor wafers to end up in the junk heap, you can't pin down the individual who just mushily reported it to save your life. Instead, you end up spending the next half-hour playing charades with the individual until the truth finally comes out.

We can't stand ambiguity in our meetings. To us, it is a sure sign that participants are either afraid to address a problem head on or are trying to pass a problem off on someone else without taking ownership of their part in the process.

---

What is a committee? A group of the unwilling, picked from the unfit, to do the unnecessary.

—Richard Harkness

Regardless of the reason for the ambiguity, it is an easy way to get nowhere fast. Instead of dealing in the specifics of a problem and quickly finding solutions, the meeting ends up becoming a cat and mouse game of hide-and-seek. This outcome does nothing but waste time.

When you encounter ambiguous participants in your meetings, the best solution is to shine as bright a light on them as possible. Stop the meeting and ask the offender to elaborate: *Exactly what are you saying? How long has this been going on? What department is causing the problem? Who exactly is involved in the problem?* Increasingly push the participant into giving concrete examples to support their vague references and allegations. Of course, it is important that you do so in a safe and supportive way—this is not an inquisition, after all. You're only trying to get to the heart of the matter as quickly as possible.

Refuse to let a meeting devolve into a pool of spineless, quivering mush. JELL-O gelatin is fine for dessert, but not for business meetings. Instead, insist on, and constantly seek, the real story from the people who attend your meetings. As they realize that this is a fundamental and consistent part of your meeting management style, the participants in your future groups will naturally begin to comply with your desires without your always having to force the issue.

## Topic Jumping

Have you ever found yourself in this situation? The meeting that you are attending is moving along smartly. You can't believe the point that John made, though. There's no way that his assertion can go by unchallenged. As you spend the next several minutes framing your response—considering the alternatives, the ramifications, and how best to make your presentation to the group—the topic jumps to something completely different, unbeknownst to and unnoticed by you. Finally, after you have distilled your thoughts down to something you are satisfied to present to the rest of the group, you quickly interject your point at the next opportunity.

The only problem is that, by the time you make your point, the discussion has gone way beyond whatever it is that you have brought up, and everyone stares at you blankly, wondering where you have been for the last ten minutes. Once again, you and your meeting team are victims of topic jumping.

To some extent, we all jump topics in our conversations with others. It is natural for us to frame responses to discussion points, and for the process to take at least some small amount of time. The problem begins when these small amounts of time become larger and larger amounts of time. It is impossible to both carefully listen to the current speaker and simultaneously plan out your next comment. You just can't do it. In trying, you end up accomplishing only two things: You fall behind the progress of the group discussion, and you lose the benefit of the discussion that you have missed.

There are a few things that meeting leaders can do to help put an end to topic jumping. First, the meeting leader should point out the occurrence of topic jumping when it starts to get out of control. Awareness of the problem can often solve it. Another way to help prevent rampant jumping is to ensure that topics are completely closed out before moving to the next item on the agenda. Finally, if one or two people are consistently offending, defuse their need to topic jump by querying them regularly to make sure they have had a chance to contribute before you move too far ahead with the meeting.

## SHARE THE WEALTH

The best leaders are those who shun the limelight and who instead take every possible opportunity to shine it squarely on their subordinates and co-workers. A leader

**EXHIBIT 5-3**
*Make Your Employees Shine*

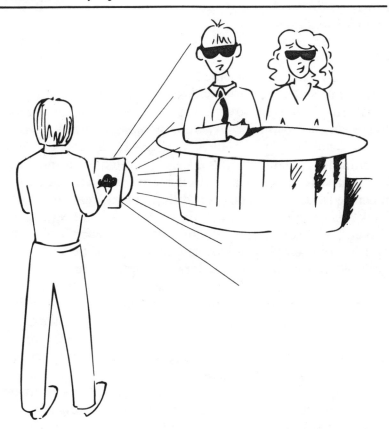

who is confident with his or her own abilities can afford
to share the wealth that comes from recognition for a job
well done. A leader who lacks self-confidence, on the
other hand, will try to hog the spotlight or, failing
that, will try to make his or her co-workers look bad by
comparison by constantly pointing out their flaws and
foibles.

In making the transition from leader to coach, the smart
meeting leader will encourage the development of leadership skill in her staff and subordinates. We all need to

grow if we are to remain a vital force in our organizations. We cannot grow, however, unless we are given the opportunity to do so. Meetings are a great place to teach and learn leadership skills.

The next time you have a meeting scheduled, consider asking one of your subordinates to lead it for you. Not only will you give your employee the opportunity to learn leadership skills, but you will also demonstrate your personal trust in the employee's capabilities. If you are willing to spread this responsibility among as many employees as you possibly can, you will have a great, inexpensive way of building staff morale. You can still attend the meeting, but you will do so as a regular team member, not as the meeting leader. It can be very different for a manager to sit back and go along for the ride when she has been in the driver's seat for so long. Unless you step back, however, and let your employee lead the meeting, he or she won't get the full benefit of the leadership opportunity.

Another option is for the manager to run the overall meeting, but break its content into distinct subparts that can then be delegated to other employees. This way, the manager can still control the overall conduct of the meeting agenda, but he can simultaneously relieve some of the burden on his personal schedule, as well as provide leadership opportunities for his subordinates. This method works particularly well in staff or training meetings.

Meetings are a great way to provide opportunities for your employees to shine. In these days of continually reduced budgets, increased layoffs, and worse, we find that we have to be much more creative in the selection of rewards for employees. In many organizations, bonus pools and the like are but distant memories from the past. Nowadays, the only bonus most of us get is one more day without a pink slip. Salary rollbacks, benefits reductions, and mandatory leave have become commonplace. As monetary reward resources have dried up, we have had to turn increasingly to nonmonetary incentives. Delegating tasks to employees, including the leadership of meetings, and then allowing your employees to bask in the recognition that comes from that success, can have much deeper, and much longer-lasting, benefits than monetary incentives ever could.

## BUILD A TEAM

We hear a lot about the importance of being team players in business. How many resumés have come across your desk over the past few years that failed to mention that the candidate was a team player. Not many, we would guess. Take a look at your own resumé. It's likely that you made a special point of announcing the importance that you attach to your own team skills. Although we are a nation built on a foundation of rugged individualists, we can also appreciate the increased utility that results from a group of individuals who function as a team.

If you look at a typical organization, you can see that there is a need for both kinds of people. The mantle of individualist initiative once worn proudly by our pioneer forebears, has now been taken over by the entrepreneurs who, at great personal financial risk, forge ahead in innovation and new enterprises. You probably have at least one or two of these people within your organization. He or she may be your founder or CEO. You may find him in charge of the research lab, or heading up your strategic planning department. Often eccentric, always thinking light years ahead of everyone else, never afraid to strike out in some new direction, the organizational individualist always surprises and never disappoints. While the individualist may fail more often than succeed, without the constant innovation and spark that he or she provides to an organization, it would surely shrivel up and die.

Just as important to good organizational health and vitality are the day-to-day efforts of team players throughout your organization. A properly functioning team is what makes an operation operate. This team of stable individuals provides both the foundation and the structure of the company. As such, we want them to be somewhat conservative, to be risk adverse, to play by the organization's rules, to cooperate fully with each other, to follow orders, and to maintain consistent work schedules.

While the entrepreneurs provide the spark, the initiative, and the direction to an organization, the rest of the team provides the glue that holds it all together. It is critical for the healthy functioning of your organization that you build teamwork and cooperation whenever and wherever you possibly can. The best team leaders understand that it takes both kinds of people to make a company run at its peak efficiency. They therefore ensure that the entrepreneurs are given enough freedom to pursue their personal agendas, while the rest of the members of the team are provided with enough structure to help them work together effectively.

# Chapter 6

# The Role of Participants

**Objectives:**

- To show that meeting participants can have a positive influence on successful meeting outcomes.
- To describe specific techniques that meeting participants can apply to help make meetings better.
- To present methods that make disagreement a positive instead of a negative factor in your meetings.

As you know by now, the heart and soul of meeting management is the transformation of group members from passive attendees to active, assertive participants. While the last chapter concentrated on the responsibilities of meeting leaders to ensure that meetings are optimized, we must now consider the responsibilities, and the power, of meeting participants. In this chapter, we will explore how any group member can use meeting management techniques to improve the meetings he or she participates in.

Meeting participants can choose to be like so much wallpaper, or they can take an active and important role in meetings. Those who choose the former route, the path of least resistance, are doomed to live through countless meetings that go nowhere. These silently suffering employees, instead of taking action to make meetings better, will grouse to anyone within earshot about how all the meetings they attend are a tremendous waste of time and how *they* would change things if they were in charge.

Well, surprise. You *are* in charge—but, now here's the catch, *only if you want to be.* Meeting leaders and your co-workers don't like wasted meetings any more than you do. As you read this chapter, consider some of the things you can do to make your meetings better. Then, at your next meeting, try out some of the techniques described in this chapter. We guarantee that, once you make a real effort to make meetings more efficient and effective, you will see the meetings you attend improve quickly and dramatically.

## EACH MEMBER AS LEADER

Sure, every meeting has a designated leader or, in some cases, leaders. Leaders provide focus and direction in the meeting and coach the other members to contribute to the overall group process. Just because a leader has been appointed to direct the meeting, however, doesn't mean that the other participants should passively sit back and wait for something to happen.

Every meeting participant can and should be a leader. This doesn't mean we are going to appoint all 10 participants in a meeting to lead it. There will still be one appointed leader. What this does mean is that we as meeting participants need to actively apply meeting leadership skills to supplement and enhance the efforts of the meeting leader to make the meeting more efficient and effective.

> But men must know, that in this theatre of man's life it is reserved only for God and angels to be lookers on.
>
> —Sir Francis Bacon

Don't wait until you are asked. If you wait until you are asked, you may never be asked. Refuse to be a passive participant! Before you agree to participate in the meeting, make a positive determination that your attendance is really required—it may not be. Too many of us attend meetings simply because we are invited. The active participant will first find out exactly what the meeting is going to be about, and then decide if she or he should attend.

In many cases, we may find that our attendance isn't really required or that one of our co-workers who knows more about the topic should attend instead. This happens to us all the time. Just because we may be in charge of the corporation's telecommunications systems, everyone assumes that we must be the resident expert, so we are invited to any and all meetings where telecommunications is one of the discussion topics. Of course, we may not be the expert; one of our assistants may be. Since he or she probably knows far more about our telecommunications than we do, we should always make a point of sending him or her in our stead. As managers, we know a little about a lot of different things. We have to learn to recognize that our employees may know a lot more about the particulars of the organization's operations than we could ever pretend to know. Instead of wasting everyone's time (including our own) with our participation, we should always make a determination whether our presence is really required and, if not, who can best speak to the issue.

You can't exert leadership in a meeting if you are unprepared. Before you participate in a meeting, make sure you get a copy of the agenda, and review it carefully. If there is no agenda available before the meeting starts, briefly discuss the planned topics with the meeting leader ahead of time. After you find out what is going to be discussed, make sure you spend some time before the meeting researching the topics and getting prepared for the meeting discussion. A sure way to kill a meeting is for the participants to be unprepared for it.

Finally, make your points, then move on. Once you have made your presentation, allow others to make theirs. If possible, as you make contributions, build upon what others have said before you. There is much to be said for the meeting participant who assertively makes his or her points, then backs off and listens to what the other meeting participants have to say. In this way, meetings truly become participative, give and take events instead of monologues. As meeting participants, we can all have a tremendous influence over the outcome of a meeting—if only we will make an effort to become active players in the meeting process.

## KEY PARTICIPANT SKILLS

As we have seen, every participant can provide leadership in a meeting—whether he or she is the appointed meeting leader or not. Simply being a participant in a meeting is not an excuse for allowing a meeting to get bogged down due to the lack of proper focus or direction.

There are many active participant skills available to us to help make our meetings better. In this section, we will discuss some of the most effective of these skills. As you read through this chapter, try to relate the different skills to how you conduct your meetings.

### Listen!

Unfortunately, despite our best efforts to the contrary, many of us don't listen to the full range of discussion that swirls around us in our daily meetings. In some cases, this is because we are too busy framing the points that we will present to the group.

✳ ✳ ✳ ✳ ✳

"I can't believe Bill said that! Now let's see . . . there must be two or three different examples that I can think of to refute his point. . . . "

In other cases, this is because we have other, more pressing matters on our minds.

"Geez! As soon as I get out of this meeting, I have to finish that proposal and get it ready for Federal Express to pick up!"

In still other cases, we may have no interest at all in the topic being discussed.

"Zzzzzzzz . . . "

✳ ✳ ✳ ✳ ✳

Active listening is hard work. Listening is not just a matter of opening your ears and waiting for the information to come pouring in. If that's all you do in the listening department, the information that comes pouring into your left ear is likely to immediately pour out of your right ear.

Take an interest in what your co-workers have to say and guard against distractions. If you don't, you are bound to miss out on some piece of important information that could be of immediate benefit to your part of the discussion or of future benefit in your business dealings. If you really aren't interested in the topic, and you find it particularly difficult to maintain your attention, then do yourself a favor and excuse yourself from the meeting so you can do something more useful. If you're not contributing to the meeting, it is much better to recognize that fact and beg off than to pretend to be a part of the process for the next two hours.

### *Participate, But Don't Dominate*

If we have a real interest in the topic, and if we have prepared ourselves adequately before the meeting starts, then we shouldn't have any problem whatsoever in being active participants in the meeting process. As participants, we need to walk a fine line between under participation in a discussion, and domination of the meeting. Whether we realize it or not, the other participants probably have a lot of good ideas, too. If you dominate the meeting, then those other ideas, which may actually be better than yours, can be lost forever.

It may be difficult at times but, as active participants in the meeting process, we should look beyond our own contributions, and ensure that our co-workers have the opportunity to contribute, too. The first way you can help is to closely monitor your own participation. Are you talking so much that no one else can get a word in edgewise? If so, concisely state your points, and then let the other participants step into the discussion. Some of us tend to state our points and then elaborate and elaborate. While extensive elaboration may be necessary when we are discussing certain complex topics, most business discussions can be conducted with simple and concise explanations. Give your business partners the benefit of the doubt; it is quite possible that they understood your point the first time you voiced it. If anyone needs more explanation, he or she will let you know.

Another method for participants to ensure they don't dominate meetings is to focus on the other participants. Are other participants dominating the discussion? If so, you can take steps to minimize the influence that these people wield over the group. Are certain participants not contributing at all? Once you have identified these group members, you can take steps to solicit their participation. A meeting where everyone focuses on him- or herself is like an archery contest played with vanishing targets. As each participant shoots his or her arrows of ideas at the other group members, the arrows never hit their targets because the other group members are too busy focusing on themselves to register the contributions of their teammates.

Finally, if all else fails, an active participant will change the meeting environment to help get the group moving. Maybe the meeting has, because of its subject matter, entered the realm of consummate boredom. Instead of falling asleep along with the rest of the group, any participant can take action to get things moving again. Perhaps a group participation exercise is in order. Maybe the group needs to take a break, or just stand up and stretch for a few moments. Perhaps a change in lighting or mood would make a positive difference. Regardless of which tack we take, anything we can do to get a meeting out of the doldrums and get participants participating will always benefit the meeting process.

## *Get Organized*

Lack of preparation leads directly to disorganized thought when we are in meetings. While we can easily fix this problem simply by researching the agenda items before the meeting starts, there is more to being organized than just knowing your stuff. The facts are one thing, but how we present these facts is another thing altogether.

Before you enter a meeting, organize your thoughts in writing. Then, as the meeting proceeds, modify or update your notes as needed. Going through this process of organization does several things to help make your meetings a success. First, just going through the process of organizing your thoughts in writing will help you to work through meeting issues to your own satisfaction—discarding ideas that don't directly support your contentions and retaining and expanding those that do. Next, your written notes provide a script you can use to directly support your points during the meeting discussions. By having a written script, you ensure that you will progress through your ideas in an organized and sequential manner, and you will also ensure that you don't accidentally forget important points. Finally, by having written notes available, you will avoid making vague or unsupported statements that don't apply to the overall theme of the meeting. We all know how easy it is to jump topics. Written notes help us avoid this problem and help us keep our meetings on track.

### Speak Up

It is a general rule of group dynamics that the ideas forwarded by participants who speak more loudly, more forcefully, and with greater urgency tend to be perceived as more important than the ideas of meeting participants who speak more quietly, more hesitantly, and with less urgency. Clearly, if we want our contributions to be noticed, we have to speak up!

And, why not say what you have on your mind? Isn't that why you are attending the meeting—to participate? One of the most important skills to have in the business world is to be able to quickly feel comfortable with a wide variety of business associates. Good salespeople certainly have a knack for this skill. As a part of their job, they have to meet and entertain a varied cross-section of business associates and clients and, whether they have known them for years—or for only a few minutes—treat them like old friends.

Some people are better at this skill than others. The best salespeople are social animals. The worst salespeople—the ones who don't last—are the ones who never really develop the necessary level of self-confidence with their associates and clients. And that is what it really comes down to: self-confidence. The greater our self-confidence, the more willing we will be to forcefully articulate our views in a group setting. It may take some of us months to be truly comfortable in a group. The development of a reasonable level of comfort is reflective of the development of our own self-confidence in that particular setting.

> A great deal of talent is lost to the world for the want of a little courage.
>
> —Sydney Smith

If we are looking for ways to improve our self-confidence, the best way possible is to be in total and unrelenting command of the facts. The easiest way to lose your self-confidence is to be caught off guard in a meeting. You can easily avoid that outcome by researching the agenda topics fully before the meeting starts. If you have any questions, do not hesitate to ask the meeting leader to provide you with more information.

If you are still uncomfortable with the prospect of actively participating in the group, it may be beneficial for you to involve yourself in one-on-one discussions with some of the other meeting participants before you find yourself in a group setting. These premeeting exercises will help you build self-confidence in a couple of ways. First, by meeting with the group members individually, outside of a group setting, you have the opportunity to get acquainted with some of your counterparts in a neutral, nonthreatening environment. Second, the relationships that you cement with your meeting counterparts allows you to rehearse your meeting script in advance of the meeting. Not only will you become more familiar with the points you plan to make, but you will also have the opportunity to hone them to a fine edge. By incorporating new, more successful points, and discarding those that do not work, you can be even more confident during the course of the meeting.

### Handle Conflict Effectively

Conflict is the natural and expected result of honest differences of opinion between individuals. Our ability to effectively handle conflict can have a significant effect on the

**EXHIBIT 6–1**
*Key Participant Skills*

---

❏ Listen!
❏ Participate, but don't dominate.
❏ Get organized.
❏ Speak up.
❏ Handle conflict effectively.

---

ultimate success or failure of our efforts in group meetings. A reasonable amount of conflict is the sign that your fellow group members are actively participating in the meeting process, but simply have different points of view. That is one reason we conduct meetings—to present and discuss multiple points of view with the ultimate goal of developing a consensus position that synthesizes the best elements of the group's point of view.

Don't run away from conflict—embrace it! Too many of us have been led to believe that conflict is bad for an organization, and that everyone should be in total agreement with everyone else on every topic. Not only is this belief erroneous, but the active squelching of healthy conflict will have far reaching, negative impacts on both the organization and the individuals in it.

The key participant skills listed above are summarized in Exhibit 6–1.

## HOW TO EFFECTIVELY INFLUENCE GROUPS

Think about the most influential person in your organization. Why is he or she so influential? Is it because he is smarter than everyone else in your organization? Or because he is so charismatic? Is her influence a result of the power and authority that she wields, or the eloquence and articulation of her speech? These and other factors influence our perception of influence. And, to a great degree, influence is a matter of perception. Although certain qualities, such as a dynamic personality, may have an almost universal effect on people, not every single person will react to a speaker in the same way.

Some of the skills we use to influence groups can be easily learned and applied. Others cannot. Some of the behavior patterns we exhibit in group settings are learned through the long process of socialization and cannot be easily broken. If these behaviors are negative, such as shyness or lack of confidence, then the individual will participate less than another participant who exhibits positive behaviors.

The result of lessened participation in a meeting is a concomitant reduction in influence over a group. You can't influence anyone if you don't communicate. And studies have shown time and time again that those who talk more have more influence—regardless of what other personality or intellectual skills or attributes they may bring to the table.

Despite the fact that it may be difficult for us to teach ourselves how to be charismatic or smarter, there are many skills that we can learn to make ourselves more influential in group meetings. The following list is by no means an exhaustive one. Make it a point to monitor your own patterns of group interaction and determine which behaviors have a positive effect on your influence and which behaviors have a negative influence. Once you have identified these different behaviors, you can take definite steps towards increasing the frequency of your positive behaviors while decreasing the frequency of your negative behaviors.

## Faster and Louder

You have no doubt experienced the passion that is generated by a meeting participant who is so excited by the topic that he can barely contain himself. His passion is so strong that he talks faster and louder—not consciously—but merely because he has so much to say about the topic and because he feels so strongly about it.

Group members who talk faster and louder are generally much more influential than their less passionate counterparts. The main reason for this is that group members who speak faster and louder tend to naturally dominate a group's talk time. And, as we have already discussed, the person or persons who dominate a meeting's talk time tend to also be the most influential in the final meeting outcomes.

Clearly, one way you can become more influential in meetings is to speak louder and faster. The key to doing this is not to just turn up the volume, but to be fully prepared and intimately familiar with the discussion topics. This knowledge will help give you the confidence to speak out in the group and to peel yourself off the wall.

## Overcome Gender-Specific Personality Traits

There is no doubt that males and females exhibit different interaction behaviors in group meetings. Take, for example, the tendency for men to interrupt speakers, and for women to refrain from interrupting speakers.

An integral part of the socialization of males is the development of the need to compete with their counterparts to have their ideas heard. It is not unusual for men to interrupt the other group members to make their points. We do this instinctively, without even noticing the fact that we do it.

Women, on the other hand, have traditionally been taught that it is rude to interrupt. There is therefore a tendency for women in meetings to wait for their turn to speak. Unfortunately, in a meeting full of males who are all interrupting each other to make their points, that turn may never come. Women often wait for their turn. Men generally take their turn.

Despite the time worn stereotypes that women always talk, and men tend not to talk, research has clearly shown this not to be the case. On average, women in a group discussion setting tend to talk roughly one-half of the amount of time that men do. What's really interesting about these findings is that the women in the group equaled or bettered their male counterparts in the following key areas: subject area expertise, verbal skills, and intelligence.

One way to overcome this problem is for the meeting leader, or any other participant, to call attention to the offending behavior, and request that the perpetrator refrain from cutting off the other participants. If this strategy doesn't work, female group members may have to be willing to take their turns, just like their male counterparts, rather than waiting for them.

### The Characteristics of the Contributions

The quantity, timing, and duration of contributions have a very direct effect on the influence of the group members who make them. Goldhammer and Shils proposed the following formula to describe this phenomenon:[1]

| Quantity of recommendations accepted by the group | ÷ | Quantity of recommendations attempted by the individual | = | Individual influence index |
|---|---|---|---|---|

If, for example, a participant makes 20 recommendations to the group, and the group accepts 5 of the recommendations, that participant's influence index would be 0.25.

A quick look at this equation shows us that there are two primary ways to increase our influence index:

❑ Increase the *quantity* of recommendations so that the probability of group acceptance is increased.

❑ Increase the *quality* of recommendations so that more of them are accepted by the group.

Either approach may be effective in increasing your influence over a group, but these two approaches differ significantly in their execution.

Increasing the quantity of recommendations could be likened to taking a shotgun approach to meetings. Instead of being concerned about the quality of our contributions, our goal is to get as many recommendations on the table as we can before the meeting ends. Through the sheer volume of our contributions, we are bound to hit at least a few targets.

The other approach for increasing our influence index is to increase the quality of our contributions. If the former approach could be equated to a shotgun, this approach is like a sniper's bullet—much more precisely aimed and much more effective. We can have only one contribution in a meeting, but it can be of such merit that it is accepted by the group, and our index of influence is 1.00.

The approach you decide to take will depend on the meeting and on your own mood or level of preparedness for the meeting. We may find that, in certain situations, we are much more effective when we maximize the number of our contributions to the group. At other times we may find that the meeting is better served by our making only a small quantity of high-quality recommendations. Be prepared to switch from one mode to another as the need arises.

## HOW TO DISAGREE

Despite all the pressures to conform that we face in our society, believe it or not, it is not a sin to disagree with the status quo. The basic American right of freedom of speech is generally considered to be the foundation of our great nation. The characteristic shared by all governments that seek to control their citizens is intolerance of dissent.

Many organizations are not much different than the government of post-Mao China or of certain neo-fascist Latin American countries. Instead of encouraging freedom of thought and expression, many companies actively discourage it. Whether the leadership in an organization recognizes it or not, no one person has all the answers and, although the corporation's conventional wisdom may support one particular point of view, that doesn't mean that there is only one *right* point of view. It takes all kinds of ideas to make an organization great.

As meeting participants, we should never be afraid to express ourselves or present ideas that we think will be of benefit to our organizations. Understandably, it may take more guts in some organizations than it takes in others. If a meeting participant truly believes in himself, however, and is willing to be an active participant in a meeting rather than a passive bump on a log, then he should never hesitate to speak his mind. The successful meeting manager will always actively seek to make contributions to the meeting process rather than allow herself to be a silent victim of the meeting process.

The question becomes not whether or not to disagree but how best to disagree. Obviously, confrontational tactics are not the best way to communicate your opposition to the status quo. Confrontation only leads to withdrawal by the other group members or to confrontation in return. Neither of these do anything to enhance the efficiency and effectiveness of meetings. Indeed, there are few better ways to cause a meeting's forward progress to come to a screeching halt.

The best approach to take when voicing disagreement is to be diplomatic. You will want to be firm yet nonconfrontational. Calmly describe the basis of your concerns, and then patiently provide the reasons why your point of view offers advantages that the other, more politically acceptable points of view, don't offer. Present data that supports your claims. Try your best to maintain a calm, neutral stance on the issues, and let your ideas speak for you. If they are good ones, their advantages will shine brightly through the haze and cobwebs of the status quo.

Above all, know when to push your points harder, and when to back off. While everyone has a right and a duty to disagree if they feel they are right, this doesn't necessarily mean that you should sacrifice yourself on the altar of truth to make your point. We have seen too many good people fall because they were *right*, and the status quo was *wrong*. In every disagreement there is a point of no return that you cross only at your own peril. This point of no return represents the apex of where the meeting leader and other participants have heard what you have to say, acknowledge it, but are ready to move on. In some cases, crossing this imaginary point may elicit only mild rebukes or the impatient glares of your co-workers. In other, more extreme cases, crossing the line of no return can earn the lucky offender a humiliating chewing-out by an irritated manager or, in the worst cases, dismissal from the firm.

It is obviously not in your interest, or in the firm's interest for you to lose your job over your pursuit of the ultimate truth. As long as your company is not breaking the law, it is generally a far better approach to make your point—as passionately as you desire—and then move on once it is clear that you are barking up the wrong tree.

While martyrdom wears well for poets and saints, it does not wear well at all for those of us in business. Although we may think that we are indispensable, many of us who thought our companies would not be able to function without us have found, much to our surprise, that they can get along just fine.

*Chapter 7*

# Mistakes to Avoid When Meeting

**Objectives:**

- To inventory and explain the most common mistakes made in business meetings.
- To provide techniques and strategies that can be applied to avoid making mistakes in meetings.
- To describe ways of recovering from meeting mistakes and how to apply the lessons learned to your future meetings.

You realistically can't expect to conduct perfect meetings every time. Since meetings are a uniquely human endeavor, they are subject to all the same foibles that accompany any other human endeavor. However, by applying active meeting management skills and by avoiding the mistakes discussed in this chapter, there is no reason you can't do significantly better than the 47 percent efficiency typical of most meetings. If you can bring the efficiency of your meeting up to a figure somewhere in the 70s or 80s, you will be doing well above average, and you will have accomplished significant and lasting gains for your organization.

The examples that follow are a brief look at some of the most critical mistakes that commonly occur in business meetings. There are certainly others. Avoid these mistakes, and you can instantly improve the efficiency and effectiveness of your meetings. Continue to make these mistakes, and you'll be hard pressed to ever get your meetings out of the doldrums of mediocrity.

## GETTING OFF THE SUBJECT

Despite our best efforts to maintain a focused discussion, topics can jump in the blink of an eye, and can be so far afield so quickly, we may have a difficult time bringing the group's focus back to the matter at hand.

The problem with getting off the subject is that, whenever it happens, meeting efficiency instantly falls to zero. For every minute of off-topic discussion with an efficiency of zero, multiply by the number of participants in the meeting. Let's say, for example, that a six-member group digresses or goes off topic for fifteen minutes during the course of a one-hour business meeting—a seemingly minor amount of time. While this may not seem like a big deal, if we multiply the lost time by the number of meeting participants, in this case six people, we can see that we have actually lost one and one-half hours of time over the course of a one-hour meeting. In a very real sense, we wasted more time during the meeting than the meeting's duration.

> As a general rule, the shorter the interval that separates us from our planned objective the longer it seems to us, because we apply to it a more minute scale of measurement, or simply because it occurs to us to measure it.
>
> —Marcel Proust

Aside from the obvious issue of lost time, there are other reasons to be concerned about getting off the subject. When a meeting gets off track, it becomes more difficult to focus on solving the problem that we are meeting to solve in the first place. While there are many reasons for a meeting to get off track, they all have the same result—the problem doesn't get solved until the meeting gets back on track.

Sometimes, meeting participants will intentionally attempt to derail a meeting. Perhaps the group member is afraid that, as a result of the discussion, some problem in his or her department will be exposed to the scrutiny and criticism of the group and will intentionally attempt to direct the group's attention towards some other issue. We have all seen this technique used time and time again.

A slight variation on this technique is the preemptive strike. Knowing that a meeting might expose the shortcomings of his department, or of his own personal management practices, the savvy manager will find a problem in someone else's department, and expose that problem before someone else has a chance to expose his problems. While this can often be an effective ploy, it does nothing to forward the progress of the meeting towards solving the issues on the meeting agenda.

In other cases, someone may change the topic because she wants to make a point about an unrelated issue, that she knows is unrelated, but is afraid she won't have the opportunity to voice in another, more appropriate forum. Since the topic, while unrelated to the main theme of the meeting, may be of intense interest to the group, it may be difficult to redirect discussion to the agenda. The authors have seen this kind of situation kill many otherwise fruitful meetings.

The group might be meeting, for example, to discuss the implementation of the pending payroll system conversion. Right in the middle of the meeting, one of the participants announces that he just got the word on how the corporate layoffs would be handled, and who was on the list. Needless to say, this topic will be of far more interest to the meeting participants than the payroll system conversion. While the topic of layoffs may be an important one to the group, its discussion will not get the group any closer to meeting its objective or getting the payroll system conversion completed on schedule.

In many cases, topic jumps are not made intentionally or in a conscious attempt to subvert the meeting process. We often get off the subject as a natural cause of wanting to pursue an idea that is interesting to us, whether or not it is immediately applicable or relevant to the subject of the meeting. Sometimes ideas just pop into our heads and, rather than lose the idea, we feel we should express it to the group. Once again, the group may find these ideas of interest but, in pursuing them during the course of the meeting, the group is doing nothing towards accomplishment of the goals that it set for itself when it originally agreed to meet.

The obvious solution to the problem of getting off the topic is for the group leader or facilitator to aggressively ensure that group discussions stay focused on the items listed on the meeting agenda. This is not to say that the off-topic ideas don't have merit—they may be tremendously important to the organization. However, if they merit discussion, they should be recorded, and future meetings should be scheduled to address them. In this way, we will ensure we recruit the best possible roster of participants to address these issues. We will also ensure that we focus all the energies of our current meeting group on solving the problems that are before us.

## NO GOALS, NO AGENDA

So, why are you calling that meeting, anyway? Do you really know why? Are your goals clear enough to you that you can sketch out a written agenda, or are they still indefinite? If we are going to go to the effort of calling a meeting and seeking the participation of our co-workers, it is essential that we know *why* we are meeting and exactly what our goals are.

We have all attended far too many meetings where it is not clear why we were meeting. After countless years of putting up with these rudderless nonevents, we can no longer passively tolerate them. For several days, I was being hounded to attend a contract-signing meeting. In the 14 years that I've been in business, I have only rarely participated in contract-signing meetings. If the contract was particularly important to the company, I would fly out to the customer's site and sign the contract, but 99 percent of the time, Federal Express or the U.S. Postal Service did the job.

**✳ ✳ ✳ ✳ ✳**

"So, Carol, why don't we just send our courier over with the contract? Our contractor will get it today and they will have several days to review it, sign it, and return it to us."

That made perfect sense to me. I just couldn't imagine why we would want to schedule a meeting to watch these guys sign the contract.

"I still think we should have a meeting, Peter. There are a number of issues that I need to clarify with them about the contract."

Now I was really confused. I had to find out the real reason for having the meeting.

"But haven't we finalized the contract language yet, Carol? If so, what's to discuss? Why don't we just get the contract to them, and have them sign and return it?"

**✳ ✳ ✳ ✳ ✳**

The problem was that my co-worker, Carol, wanted to have a meeting, but she had no clear idea why. Just a knee-jerk desire to hold a meeting when none was required. And, I wasn't about to get roped into a meeting with no clear reason to meet.

It's sort of like the lesson we learned after fighting for the better part of a decade in the steamy, far away jungles of Southeast Asia. While we knew that we were there to fight the communist "menace," we didn't have clear goals or objectives. Instead of a quick and tidy victory, we ended up in a quagmire of monumental proportions. The lessons from our Vietnam experience can be applied to our meetings. If the reasons for having the meeting are not crystal-clear, and if the objectives are not elucidated in advance, then seriously consider refusing to participate in the meeting, or at least help your co-worker define his agenda so that he is satisfied with the need for meeting.

This is especially important for meetings that are highly directive in nature. Brainstorming meetings are, by nature, less dependent on an agenda. Training meetings, on the other hand, are almost impossible to conduct without one. Even brainstorming meetings need to have a general framework of goals and objectives before they start. That is where a well thought-out and complete agenda can be of real benefit to the success of a meeting.

## MEETING TOO LONG

Can you still remember the fundamental axiom of meeting management? Here it is one last time.

> End the meeting the moment the objectives are achieved or when progress towards meeting them ceases.

Recent surveys of management and technical professionals have shown that one of the most frequently cited meeting problems is that they last too long. The reasons for this problem are many and varied. All of these reasons, regardless of their source, can lead to two things—increased frustration on the part of meeting participants and, ultimately, the failure of the meeting to reach its goals. So why do meetings last so long, anyway? One reason is that we may have invited the wrong people to participate in our meeting. For a meeting to be as efficient and effective as possible, we have to have the right people on our meeting team. We may have a great reason to meet, and we may have an amazing agenda, but if the people in our meeting don't know anything about what we are going to talk about or, worse, don't care, then it is just not going to work.

Another reason meetings last too long is that some meeting leaders get lax in enforcing meeting start times. One of the authors used to be involved in a regular, weekly quality meeting for several months as a group facilitator. The meeting was scheduled for 10:00 A.M. every Tuesday. However, regardless of the agreed-upon meeting time, the meeting leader never arrived before 10:15 A.M. Of course, since the meeting got started late, the leader always insisted that the meeting continue past the 11:00 A.M. scheduled ending time. The author always showed up on time—ready to work. After staying late a couple of times, he wised up and started walking out of the meetings precisely at 11:00 A.M., regardless of where the meeting team was in its proceedings. He even suggested to the meeting leader that she try starting the meetings on time but, alas, to no avail.

Jimmy Williams, the CEO of SunTrust, was reported by *Fortune* to be a strong believer in meetings that start on time. When meeting attendees are late, Williams says, "I say very politely, I was here at 9. I'm sorry you were late. But I'm going to have to leave on schedule at 9:30."[1] Not only does that message speed up the meeting, but it makes the participants think twice about showing up late again.

**EXHIBIT 7–1**
*Start Your Meeting on Time!*

If you start a meeting late, that doesn't mean you shouldn't still end the meeting on time. It's unlikely that the work schedules of your fellow group members revolve around your meeting. Don't forget that they probably have other business to attend to and keeping them late will only make them anxious and distract your meeting team from the task at hand.

Sometimes we just don't know when to give it up. We have to realize that not every meeting is going to result in a successful conclusion. It may be that the problem is far more complex than we originally imagined, or the problems are systemic and beyond the scope of our group. Quite possibly, we have not achieved the critical mass necessary to solve the particular issues on our agenda.

If your meeting is not successful, you have to be able to recognize that fact, and then quickly bring the meeting to a close. Some people, instead of gracefully retreating, will pour in still more resources, hoping for some sort of breakthrough. While this strategy may occasionally be an effective one, more often than not it just means that more time will be wasted by more people. No matter how hard you try, some meetings are just not meant to be. Don't take it personally, and don't view it as a failure. The real failure would be if you continued to meet long after it has become apparent that there is no longer any reason to meet.

Don't lose any sleep about it. Reconsider your objectives, draw up a new agenda, and a new list of attendees. Try again. Perhaps the next time will be the charm.

## LACK OF PREPARATION

There is no excuse for being unprepared for a business meeting. Well, maybe one. If you're not on your deathbed, however, you are going to have a hard time convincing us that you can't spend at least a few minutes before a meeting preparing for it.

The big problem with the lack of preparation for meetings is that either lots of time will be wasted as we feel our way around the topics, or the meeting will come to a grinding halt when someone figures out we don't have any idea what we are talking about. This last situation can have disastrous results.

Take, for example, a situation where the chief executive officer of a large, multinational corporation, John, has called a meeting to determine why sales are dropping so precipitously in the western region. All the hot shots are there. There is a nervous tension in the air because everyone knows that the CEO is not a happy camper. He wants answers, and he wants them now.

# ✳ ✳ ✳ ✳ ✳

"I think you all know why you're here today. I have called this meeting to address the rapid decline in western region sales over the last fiscal quarter. Our profit margins are already slim this year. We cannot afford any further drops in revenues. Susan, would you please describe the full extent of the problem?"

The company's chief financial officer, Susan, rises to speak. "Thank you, John. As you can see from the charts that Mark is passing around the room (Exhibit 7–2), the 3rd quarter sales are down substantially from the figures for the 2nd quarter. This represents a dramatic decline from the same period last fiscal year."

John chimes in. "All right. We have seen the ugly numbers. Now, I want to know what the problem is and how we are going to solve it. Cathy, you are in charge of marketing, what's going on out there?"

Cathy rises to speak. "I wish I knew, John. These numbers do not make sense to me. I am positive that we are hitting our sales goals. I just can't imagine what the problem is."

John interrupts. "Come on, Cathy. There has got to be a reason. You can't get numbers like that without there being an obvious problem in your sales organization!"

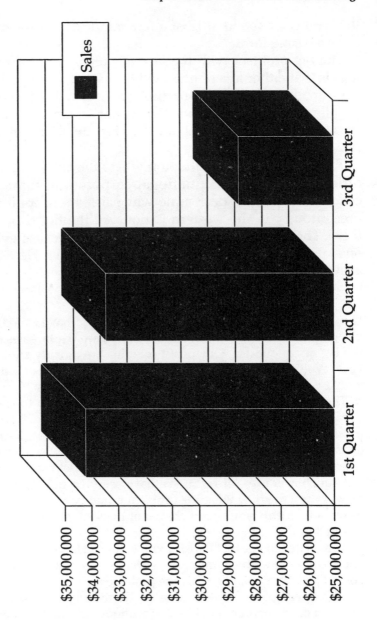

While the CEO is raking her over the coals, Cathy takes a closer look at the chart and notices a problem.

"Susan, are you sure these numbers are correct? From what I can tell, these figures don't include those two big orders that we landed on September 29th. Are you absolutely sure that you counted those orders in your sales figures?"

Susan responds. "Yeah, I'm sure that we included all your booked 3rd quarter orders. Wait a minute. Mark prepared the reports. Let's get it straight from the horse's mouth."

Mark fumbles through his notes, then answers sheepishly. "What orders are you talking about? I don't show any activity at all in the last week of September."

Now, John, the chief executive officer, is really fuming. "What? You mean to tell me that you don't know if these charts are correct or not? I can't believe it! Get back to your office right now and get me some numbers I can rely on! This meeting is over until you get your act together!"

## ✳ ✳ ✳ ✳ ✳

At a minimum, the lack of preparation can lead to meeting inefficiency as the participants get up to speed on the topics. At its worst, the lack of preparation can destroy the progress that has been made in a meeting, or even torpedo the credibility of the meeting participants. Take at least a few minutes before every meeting to prepare. You will make your meetings more efficient and perhaps you will save yourself embarrassment.

## AMBIGUOUS RESULTS

Ambiguous results rarely solve an issue. Instead, they often lead to repetition of the problem, which necessitates further meetings to attempt to solve it again. For a meeting to be considered effective, the recommendations that result from the meeting process must be complete, well-defined, and unambiguous.

Ambiguous recommendations are often the result of a meeting group that either does not fully understand the problem or is afraid for whatever reason to address the problem head-on. Whatever the cause of ambiguous results, they should not be tolerated in meetings you attend. Whether you are a meeting leader or a meeting participant, there are positive steps you can take to ensure that the outcomes of your meetings are clear, understandable, and have real meaning to your organization.

> The pretext for indecisiveness is commonly mature deliberation; but in reality indecisive men occupy themselves less in deliberation than others; for to him who fears to decide, deliberation (which has a foretaste of fear) soon becomes intolerably irksome, and the mind escapes from the anxiety of it into alien themes.
>
> —Sir Henry Taylor

If, for example, a group is not properly prepared in advance of the meeting to discuss all of the details regarding all of the issues surrounding all of the items on the agenda, it will be difficult, at best, for the group to reach meaningful results that satisfy all aspects of the agenda. Sure, the group might have success with certain topics; however, others will be only partly satisfied, and still others will be ignored altogether. A group leader should, whenever possible, issue a formal, written agenda in advance of the meeting so that the attendees will have some idea what they are to prepare for. Don't wait until the last minute, however. Some meeting leaders think it sufficient to place copies of the agenda in the participants' in-boxes fifteen minutes before the meeting is to start. While it's good that she has completed an agenda, the manager is not leveraging all the benefits of the agenda to her best advantage.

The meeting participant's role is then to *read* the agenda in advance of the meeting and then do whatever research is necessary to be fully prepared. We still have problems getting participants in our meetings to read the agenda before they set foot in the room. It only takes one participant who hasn't prepared for the meeting to cause the productivity of the rest of the group to go into the tank. How many times have you sat through a meeting where every issue had to be explained at great length to someone who obviously had no idea what was going on?

One more technique we have found to be of value is to identify the participants who may need some extra coaching, tutoring, or assistance before they attend the meeting. It really pays off to spend some one-on-one time with these people so that they can become full-fledged members of the group process. Not only do you achieve the benefit of cutting loose potential group boat anchors, but you also help to ensure that everyone in the meeting actively participates. Active, informed participation by all group members is one of the best ways to prevent ambiguous outcomes. While you can't always lead your group members to water and expect them to drink, you *can* ensure that they will have the opportunity to drink.

All too often, one or more meeting participants live in mortal fear of rocking the corporate boat. Perhaps afraid that they will lose their jobs or afraid of confrontation or maybe just afraid to take a stand on any issue of any substance, some participants simply try to survive meetings without once opening their mouths. Like so much corporate wallpaper, these group members spend the entire meeting hoping that they won't be noticed.

Unfortunately, people who try out their impersonations of wallpaper in your meetings do nothing to enhance the meeting outcomes. While their participation, or lack thereof, may seem innocent enough—simply a waste of time—the real problem is when fearful participants *actively* attempt to steer the group into making ambiguous decisions, or producing ambiguous outcomes. Why would anyone want a meeting to end in ambiguity?

Every organization is populated by a wide variety of personality types. Some employees are passive, while others are aggressive. Some are conservative, while others are risk takers. Some are team players, while others are lone wolves. Some employees are bold, while others are timid. Every vital, growing organization needs a mix of all of these personality types to function well. An organization quickly becomes dysfunctional, however, when one of these personality types dominates at the expense of the others.

If fear is pervasive throughout an organization, the results of meetings will naturally reflect the fear of the individuals who are a part of the meeting process. Some managers feel that the best way to run their organizations is through fear. They bark out orders to their subordinates, they leave them in the dark, they assign them impossible tasks with impossible deadlines, and they publicly humiliate their employees for daring to tell the truth. While managers who use fear as a motivator may see short-term gains, they fail to realize that, in the long term, they are undermining the foundation of trust, loyalty, and risk taking that enables an organization to excel. In the organization ruled by fear, new ideas are discouraged, unless they are brought forward by the leadership team. Prudent risk taking, instead of being rewarded, is punished. In the place of a climate that supports growth and innovation, we find an organization steeped in an atmosphere of fear and mistrust. As a result, ambiguity is its own reward, and clear, decisive action is reserved only for the members of the ruling elite.

Again, do everything in your power to guard against ambiguous meeting results and outcomes. Such results only lead to confusion and uncertainty among most of the group members and, inevitably, to a need to address the issue again and again until it finally goes away. Take positive steps, such as issuing agendas in advance with individuals responsible for each agenda item or by personally contacting less informed group members. If participants are fearful of making comments or decisions that may be in conflict with the prevailing conventional wisdom, get to the root of that fear, and take steps to identify and defuse it.

## KEY PLAYERS MISSING IN ACTION

A lot of people go to a lot of trouble to put meetings together, only to have them fail due to nonattendance by one or more critical players or stakeholders. Perhaps due to conflicting priorities or perhaps due to forgetfulness, whatever the reason, if a key player is missing, your meeting may be doomed to failure before it starts.

While, in an ideal world, it might be nice to think that all participants in your meetings are equally important to realizing successful outcomes, the reality is that some participants are more equal than others. And, while the loss of a less important player might not be missed, the loss of a key player may dramatically affect the results of the meeting or the ultimate buy-in by the stakeholders in the recommendations made by the meeting participants.

When you lose the participation of key players, you have to make a decision whether to continue with the meeting, knowing that the meeting outcomes may be less than optimal, or to cancel the meeting outright and reschedule it. If it is unlikely that the meeting will be successful if one or more key players are absent, then you should postpone it. It is far better to try again later than to risk wasting the time spent by all the other meeting participants grappling for a solution that can't be found without the active participation of the key participants.

To help maximize the attendance by all meeting participants, send out reminders before you meet, or personally call each of the participants to confirm their attendance. As busy as we all are, we can easily lose meetings in our full schedules. By taking a little extra time out of our own schedules, and by following up with the key players to ensure their attendance, we can guarantee that our meetings will be more efficient, more effective, and that their outcomes will be consistently better than average.

## DICTATORSHIP OF THE FEW

We have all participated in meetings where one or two people dominated at the expense of the participation of the other members of the group. It is rare that dictatorship by the few results in better meeting outcomes. More often than not, the results are frustrated team members and outcomes that are incomplete and skewed towards one particular point of view.

Some people dominate meetings through the sheer force of their personalities. Others dominate because they are more knowledgeable about a particular topic than the other participants. Still other participants dominate by default due to the nonparticipation of the other group members.

> We are more anxious to speak than to be heard.
>
> —Thoreau

Regardless of the reasons for dictatorship by the few in group meetings, the result is the same—less efficient, less effective meetings. A key task for the meeting leader is to ensure relative parity of talk time among all participants. This means taking an active orientation towards meeting management. The meeting leader cannot sit passively back and allow certain participants to dominate. For a meeting to be successful, the leader has to support and encourage the participation of members who seem less willing to participate and, at times, intercede to minimize the domination of a meeting by particular members.

There are different ways for a meeting leader to take charge of those who would dominate the proceedings. Some methods are subtle, others are anything but. One way to take charge of the situation is to thank the overzealous participant for his input, and ask him to allow the other participants to have a chance to express their views. At the same time, you have to solicit the participation of the other members; otherwise, there will be a vacuum in the discussion that the dominant participants will quickly move to fill.

If the dominant group members refuse, after your gentle persuasions, to back off and allow others to participate, you will have to be more persistent and more forceful in your efforts. If, after repeated efforts to tone down a meeting dominator, you still can't control his input, then take the offender aside and explain that you will not tolerate his behavior and that continued abuse of the other meeting participants' talk time will result in his ejection from the meeting. Don't be afraid to request a meeting dominator to step out of a meeting if necessary. While you may feel uncomfortable doing so, the comfort and the contributions of all the other meeting participants will be greatly increased by ridding the meeting of the few troublemakers who would rather dominate than participate.

# Chapter 8

# Valuing Our Differences

**Objectives:**

- To describe the very real benefits of inclusion of staff input versus exclusion.
- To explore the nature of our differences.
- To provide effective tools for eliciting the full participation of all employees.

Until fairly recently, the ranks of American business management were dominated by white, able-bodied, Anglo-Saxon, Protestant males. This is no longer the case. With each passing year, more women, more people of color, and more physically challenged people are being hired and promoted to positions of power, influence, and importance in American business. While there is still a long way to go before true parity for all groups is established (one study, for example, predicts that women will not reach parity in the executive ranks of American business until the year 2466—472 years from now[1]), the "good old boy" networks that so dominated business in the past are slowly dying away.

Accompanying this shift in the demographics of corporate America, more managers are beginning to recognize the importance of utilizing multicultural work groups to develop alternatives and solutions to problems. Instead of making decisions in isolation with only limited, controlled input, the wisdom of soliciting and seriously considering a wide variety of opinion has become apparent to an increasing number of us. Considering diversity of opinion increases the number of options available to us and, by broadening the group's experience base, strengthens the evaluation of each option. If we seriously solicit and value the opinions of *all* those who work for us, we can expect happier, more productive employees as a result. For those willing to take the time, valuing differences can clearly provide a competitive advantage in the marketplace.

The trend towards inclusion has had a definite impact on the dynamics of meetings. All participants must now consider the unique point of view of other meeting participants—each of whom has his or her perspective to bring to the table. While there is certainly more that unites than separates us, we have our own unique perspective shaped by our life experience. Those individuals who have grown-up in the African-American culture, for example, clearly have a perspective different than those of us who are a part of an Asian culture. It is the wise business person who constantly seeks out avenues that tap these diverse perspectives. Meetings are an extraordinarily effective way of accomplishing this goal.

## THE GOOD OLD BOYS

To maintain control and accountability, managers have traditionally oriented businesses around a strict, authoritarian organizational model. This model left little room for employee participation in the decision-making process. And, since the reins of power were typically held by Caucasian males, everyone else was traditionally denied access to the decision-making process.

Despite the introduction of newer, participative styles of management and decision making, some organizations still rely on authoritarian techniques to maintain control over the actions of employees. The care and feeding of employee fear through the threat of demotion, reassignment, or firing is the implicit task of many high-level managers. Notwithstanding their protests to the contrary, many individuals in top management positions feel that certain decisions are strictly theirs to make, and that it would be a gross abdication of their responsibilities if they empowered employees at lower levels to make the decisions that are most critical to the organization.

> Men in high places, from having less personal interest in the characters of others—being safe from them— are commonly less acute observers, and with their progressive elevation in life become, as more and more indifferent to what other men are, so more and more ignorant of them.
>
> —Sir Henry Taylor

A typical example of this situation is the drafting of an organizational vision statement. If your organization has a vision statement, who wrote it? Were employees invited to submit their ideas, and were they seriously considered? Was a special committee appointed to draft the organization's vision? Was the job relegated to the management or executive ranks? Chances are, it was written by the founders, chief executive officer, or top management group of your company in the firm belief that their vision should drive all employee efforts. It's their company after all, right?

Stated in its most simple terms, the need of all employees to feel an important and necessary role in the decision-making process, and the need of managers to control key aspects of the decision-making process, are often in direct conflict. Unfortunately, this inherent conflict is very much a part of the fundamental framework of the majority of American business organizations. To date, most organizations have emphasized division of labor, functional specialization of tasks, and full and complete accountability of individuals in their work. Dating back to the model of the Roman army, all power flows down through the organization from the top. Only in limited situations can we fully delegate decisions to individuals in the lower ranks of an organization. The most prevalent American organizational model has managers making the most important decisions with little or no real delegation to those most affected by those decisions. While many managers may ask for the input, opinions, or recommendations of their subordinates, most still make the final, organizational life-or-death decisions on their own.

Most employees—regardless of their race, gender, or socioeconomic status—want and need to be a part of the decision-making process in their workplace. Employees report that they are more satisfied with and more committed to a decision that they have had a part in framing. Organizations that ignore this fact are inviting lowered employee productivity, decreased motivation, and lessened commitment. While there are some individuals who prefer, and indeed thrive, in a highly directive environment, the rule is that most employees want to play an integral part in the activities that most affect their jobs.

So, how does this innate conflict specifically affect business meetings? To begin, each time we make a decision without the input of all stakeholders or expert members of the group, conflict is likely to result. The kind of distrust that results from this circumstance not only undercuts the decision that is made, but it also undercuts the decisions that are made in other meetings, as well as the perceived authority of the management team. When we give individuals false expectations of their role in the decision-making process, participants often feel betrayed, confused, and resentful when they are then excluded from the process. Over time, participants experience these feelings not only toward the meeting leader, but towards the organization in general.

Since the small group is the primary forum for business meetings, this is where the drama plays out, and this is where an organization can make its greatest impact on the organization. While many individuals in organizations may be content with the status quo and the full range of resultant negative effects on the organization, smart individuals will make every effort to use meetings to equalize information and ownership and distribute the responsibility for decision making throughout the organization.

## THE NATURE OF OUR DIFFERENCES

Many people object to the recent focus on diversity and the attendant focus on the differences between us rather than focusing our similarities. Some people feel that, by explicitly recognizing our differences, we will further polarize our workforce rather than draw it together.

It is our sincere belief that, to fully tap the potential of *every* individual in our organizations, we have no choice but to be sensitive to the unique needs that each of our employees, clients, or other business associates brings to the table. In some cases, these unique needs may be a result of race- or cultural-driven factors. In other cases, these unique needs may be gender- or age-driven. Regardless of the root of our differences, to ignore them is to ignore the full potential of our colleagues.

## *Gender-Specific Differences*

Of all the characteristics that make us different from each other, gender is probably the most fundamental and the most physically and behaviorally obvious. And, despite the fact that women represent roughly 51 percent of the population in the United States, and almost 60 percent of all women over 18 are in the workforce (compared to 75 percent of men over 18),[2] recent studies show that women are still woefully underrepresented in the higher ranks of American business management.

A survey of Fortune 500 and Service 500 CEOs and human resource professionals disclosed that women represent less than 5 percent of senior managers in most of the respondent firms. Perhaps not surprisingly, given this result, the same survey found that women comprise 25 percent or less of "high potential employees" in the respondent firms.[3]

How do these facts affect our meetings? As shown by the above statistics, women have traditionally been relegated to lower-paid, lower-responsibility positions within most companies. We have seen the pattern repeatedly throughout our careers—men tend to gravitate to top management, while women tend to dead-end in low-status clerical jobs. There are notable exceptions to this general rule, of course, but the effect of the under representation of women in management is widespread and pervasive. The ultimate result is the exclusion of women from formal and informal work groups and from decision-making meetings. It is up to all of us to recognize this disparity, and to take steps to overcome it.

> A woman's guess is much more accurate than a man's certainty.
>
> —Rudyard Kipling

One of the first things we must realize is that men and women, for all intents and purposes, are brought up in entirely different cultures. As a result, men and women exhibit different behaviors in their interpersonal interactions. Men, who grow up playing in hierarchical groups, tend to be competitive and very concerned about their relative status in social and business interactions. Women, who tend to grow up playing in nonhierarchical groups, are generally concerned about being liked and about preserving group harmony through compromise. The net result is that men tend to naturally dominate meetings, while women tend to secondary roles—avoiding conflict by agreeing with their counterparts or by evading contentious issues altogether.

The savvy group leader will recognize these differences in the way that men and women interact in meetings, and make every attempt to bring all participants into some measure of parity. This may mean that the group leader will work hard to ensure that the male participants don't dominate the meetings, while working equally hard to ensure that the female participants are supported in their efforts to be heard by the group.

When women are left out of meetings, we lose the benefit of their expertise and of their unique point of view. Not only do we lose the benefit of their input, we also help to reinforce the exclusion of women from formal and informal work groups within our businesses. This only serves to perpetuate the low status of women in American business.

Meeting leaders have a very real opportunity to ensure that women are encouraged to be full-fledged members of their organizations—it only takes a little extra effort. The benefits to the organization are very real and quite substantial. We can no longer afford to ignore the perspective of one-half of our population. America's best corporations are taking positive steps to change the status quo. So should we all.

## Race-Related Factors

Of all the characteristics that make us different from each other, on the surface race is one of the most divisive. It isn't all that long ago that segregation of the races was considered a normal part of American life. And, although the legal structures maintaining separation of the races in America were substantially dismantled in the 1960s, the remnants of centuries of segregation, subjugation, and discrimination linger on. Today, the intent may be less conscious, and the methods more subtle, but discrimination is still a very real part of our lives.

Indeed, studies have shown that people of color have a much more difficult time making their way up the corporate ladder than do their white co-workers. One study found that the social behavior and ability of black managers to fit into the established corporate social order was a very important factor in their performance evaluation. The researchers also found, however, that this factor was not important in the evaluation of the performance of white managers.[4] These results are not surprising since American corporate culture is primarily a white corporate culture.

Stereotypes abound for application to the various ethnic groups we are likely to encounter in this country. Each ethnic group is saddled with its own set of stereotypes. We all tend to filter incoming sensory data and then match it to data that already exists from our life's set of experiences. Stereotypes provide a convenient form of shorthand for our minds. Instead of taking the time to discover the unique personality and attributes of each new person we meet, we often take one look at him or her, and then make a snap judgment as to what he or she is about. This might have been fine when we lived in caves, and we had to identify and classify a threat in time to prevent our being eaten by it, but racial stereotypes do nothing to tell us what is *inside* another person.

Make it your job to seek out and involve employees of all races in your meetings. To exclude a certain group because of some preconceived notion on your part that is based on stereotypes rather than on hard facts would indeed be unfortunate. Not only will inclusion of people of color be of direct benefit to the organization by increasing the diversity of opinion that is generated in your meetings, but inclusion will dramatically increase the satisfaction of the included employees. Rather than trying to manage disenfranchised employees of color, you will be able to gain their trust and confidence, and make them fully contributing members of your work teams.

### Cultural Factors

International meetings can put a very interesting spin on the nature of our differences. In international meetings, culture becomes the overriding issue—and the key determinant of interpersonal relations. In the world of international business, it is still very much a man's world. In some countries, Japan, for example, women are *very* rare in the ranks of management. In some Arab countries such as Saudi Arabia, women are effectively banned from participating in business altogether. Now, imagine that you are an American woman who has been sent to one of these countries to participate in a meeting. And you thought you had a tough time proving your abilities to your co-workers in *America*.

Woe to the American business person prejudiced against blacks who gets sent to an African country—Nigeria, for example—to participate in a meeting. In Nigeria, whites are a minority, and any note of condescension or arrogance on his or her part will disrupt effective communication.

Every culture has its own unique set of behaviors and characteristics. In most Asian countries, for example, it is considered very bad form to try to rush an agreement.

Asian business people put greater value in the development of a personal relationship with those with whom they conduct business than in the business itself. Many books have been written on the importance of adhering to the etiquette demanded by members of different cultural groups when conducting business or participating in meetings. It is not the intent of the authors to chronicle all of these unique cultural differences, but merely to highlight the fact that they exist and that they have to be considered when participating in international meetings.

If you have been tapped to participate in an international meeting, the best thing you can do is to thoroughly research the cultural and business etiquette of the country or countries that you will be visiting. You may be surprised to find how important such seemingly innocuous factors such as who you address your comments to or how the seating is arranged can be on the ultimate success of your meetings.

Above all, be extremely respectful of those you meet with. The term *ugly American* is the result of more than a few Americans who refused to show their hosts the respect that they deserved. Don't be too eager to demand results. Allow yourself plenty of time to develop relationships with your hosts—even though management back at home may be pressing you to close a deal as soon as possible. If you are brash and aggressive, tone down your act! If you like to hear yourself talk, take the time to listen to others. If you have a hard time adjusting to alien environments, try to seek out the unique pleasures of the new world around you.

A meeting can be a great opportunity to experience another culture. Since you are the outsider, be sure to let your host take the lead, and don't be too quick to push for tangible outcomes. The relationships you develop can be very strong and very long lasting. The benefits to your organization can be considerable.

### Other Factors

While the above factors are probably the most obvious differences between us, there are certainly others. Age, physical ability, religious affiliation, and sexual preference are but a few. Regardless of the specific attribute that factors into our perception of another person, it would be a terrible mistake to ignore the potential contributions of *any* member of our team. Refuse to allow the seeds of prejudice to plant themselves in your organization. You can make a difference! At times you may feel you are fighting the corporate tide of ignorance by yourself, but your actions will provide a shining example to other managers as you assemble a high-performing work team that includes a diverse membership.

## MEETING TECHNIQUES THAT CAPTURE AND VALUE OUR DIFFERENCES

It takes a concerted effort by a meeting leader to include real diversity of opinion in his or her meetings. It's basic human nature to surround ourselves with people like ourselves. If we aren't careful, however, we can end up with homogenous groups of yes-men and yes-women in our meetings. The result of this unfortunate circumstance can be groupthink, inadequate input, and bad decision making.

If you are sincerely interested in plugging in to the wellspring of creativity within your organization, there are several techniques that can go a long way to help you meet your goals. These techniques *do* work because they ensure that all opinions have a fair chance to be voiced and to be heard.

### Prework

Rather than inviting people to your meetings and then surprising them with your inquiries, it can be extremely beneficial to assign tasks to specific participants before the meeting starts. This *prework* will give your participants a chance to familiarize themselves with the subject matter of the meeting in advance.

The net result is that participants will be better prepared for the meeting and therefore more confident in their knowledge of meeting topics. With this knowledge, built on a firm foundation of preparation, even your least confident participants will have all the tools necessary to contribute to the meeting.

## Rotated Presentations

It's not uncommon for certain participants to actively contribute to the meeting and for other participants to barely say a word. In this case, it is important that the meeting leader find some way to engage *all* participants in the discussion.

Rotated presentations can be a very effective tactic for enlisting the participation of even your least vocal colleague. The idea is to make assignments to your team members before the meeting. For example, a typical assignment might be to compile sales data for the last fiscal year. The selected participants then present their findings in the meeting.

Rotating presentations among meeting participants can be a real confidence builder for those people who normally don't get a chance to speak up in meetings. It's like anything else—the more often you do it, the better you get. For those who have traditionally been left out of the organizational hierarchy, meeting presentations can be a very effective first step on the road to inclusion.

## Beginning with Minority Opinion

When most of us conduct meetings, we have a tendency to focus on the most frequently or the most vocally stated opinions. By doing so, we can ignore the opinions of the silent minority of participants who perhaps are not as vocal or who do not have the status or credibility that the other participants have. Unfortunately, by ignoring minority opinion, we may very well miss out on the best solutions to our problems.

If you really want to shake things up, give this a try. Instead of focusing on the majority opinions, that is, those opinions most commonly voiced by the group, start out your meeting soliciting only the opinions that are held by a minority of the participants. Don't allow anyone to interrupt their contributions. You may be surprised to find that your formerly silent minority has a lot more to say than you ever suspected.

## PSEUDO-INCLUSIONARY TACTICS

The formerly pervasive power of organizational hierarchy has taken some fairly heavy hits over the past decade. The old-style organization required that recommendations (in fact, most communication) be passed up a long chain of command to the top, with decisions being relayed back down the same, long chain of command. This style of doing business, for obvious reasons, was not conducive to rapid communication and decision making. While it may appear on the surface that long chains of command are inclusionary, they are actually quite exclusionary by concentrating real decision making in the hands of only a few key managers or executives.

The flattening of the hierarchy in modern organizations has allowed the involvement of many more individuals farther down the chain of command. For example, newly thriving Wal-Mart has four levels, from cashier to the owner. Sears, on the other hand, was until very recently under the influence of 14 levels of bureaucracy. Not only has flattening hierarchies resulted in more rapid communication and organizational response, but it has also resulted in better decision making.

In his management seminars, Tom Peters often cites the following example of decision making within the Union Pacific Railroad. It used to be that, if a Union Pacific track inspector found a problem with a customer's railroad tracks that required repair, the inspector had to relay the information up and down an elaborate chain of command within his organization before transmission to the customer. The track inspector would make his recommendation to the local track supervisor, who would report the recommendation to the yard master. He, in turn, would pass the recommendation up to the assistant train master, who would notify the train master. The train master would pass the information up to the division superintendent for transportation, who would in turn pass the information on to the division superintendent. The division superintendent would forward the recommendation up to the regional transportation superintendent, who would transmit the recommendation up to the assistant general manager, who would finally pass it on to the general manager.

Now, bear with us. The general manager would transmit the information laterally over to the assistant vice president of sales, who would pass it down to the regional sales manager. The regional sales manager in turn passed the recommendation down to the district sales manager, who would assign it to the appropriate sales representative. The sales representative would then contact the customer—if he hadn't retired yet!

In 1990, Union Pacific completely reorganized their operations—reducing their eight levels of middle management to three and laying off 900 middle managers in the process. As a result of this organizational shake-up, Union Pacific decided to let the local track inspectors take their recommendations directly to the customer— bypassing a ridiculous amount of red tape, and resulting in *much* quicker response times.[5] The trend toward flat organizational structures has been going on for some

**EXHIBIT 8–1**
*The Best Communication Is Direct Communication*

time now. Since decisions are being made at lower levels
in the organization, persuasion, not authority, is more
important in persuading co-workers to cooperate. Also,
by lowering the level at which decisions are being made,
a wider cross-section of employees are included in the
decision-making process.

By drawing together work groups, sections, or departments, and allowing them a real opportunity to participate in the decision-making process, we create teams that, as they continue to work together in common cause, begin to make more informed and, ultimately, better decisions. For a fundamental and long-lasting difference to be made in an organization, these meetings have to be ongoing—not just isolated events—and fully supported by the organization's top management.

While many people tend to think of inclusionary, participative management as a uniquely Japanese phenomenon, American industry actually has a long history of this practice. The Scanlon plan, which was one of the first experiments in participative management, was an American innovation. Named after its developer, Joe Scanlon, a member of the United Steel Workers Union, the Scanlon Plan was an organized system for soliciting worker suggestions and then rewarding them with a portion of the profit and cost savings that resulted. Developed in the days of the Great Depression, the Scanlon Plan found its way into many industries besides the steel industry that it was originally designed for.

There were three key reasons behind the development of participative management techniques. The first reason was the belief that, by providing opportunities for meaningful involvement in the decision-making process, the morale of employees who participated would be enhanced. The second reason was the belief that, since subordinate personnel were often the closest to the issues being decided, their involvement in the decision-making process would result in better overall decisions. The third reason was the hope that employee suggestions would lead to lowered costs and increased profitability.

It has been shown that the quality of decisions made in a participative process is superior to the quality of decisions made through a nonparticipative process. The reason for

this is simple—participative management allows a larger
and wider variety of information from a much greater variety of sources than does nonparticipative management.
The more information that is available, the higher the
probability that a quality decision will be made. In short,
none of us is smarter than *all of us!*

---

The way to get things done is not to mind who gets
the credit of doing them.

—Benjamin Jowett

---

We know from personal experience that, in general, the
morale of most employees increases as the extent to
which they have the opportunity to make decisions regarding matters directly affecting the scope of their duties
is increased. Of course, there are always employees who
prefer decisions to be made for them. But even these employees appreciate being given the opportunity to voice
their opinions and to be considered valuable members of
the organization.

One of the easiest ways to cause morale in an organization to plummet is to disregard the opinions and advice of
your employees. The value of this lesson shows up in the
steady growth in the use of participative management
techniques in American business over the past several
years. Skilled employees demand a voice in their organizations. It is the foolish manager who chooses to ignore the
input of his employees. Not only will he lose the benefit of
a wide variety of good ideas, but he will eventually find
his employees requesting transfers to work for more enlightened managers or simply finding jobs in other firms.

It takes more than a few meetings to create an environment that supports the kind of organizational paradigm shifts that lead to quality decision making. It requires an ongoing commitment from management and employees at all levels of the organization, starting at the top. Every meeting should provide a safe environment for the open brainstorming and discussion of ideas—no matter how off-the-wall they might appear at first glance. And, when it is time to make a decision, all meetings must grant all the resources and time necessary to make the best decisions possible, as well as the authority to implement those decisions.

## GAINING A COMPETITIVE ADVANTAGE

The more satisfied your workforce is, the more likely it is that you can use this asset to gain a real competitive advantage in the marketplace. While many factors affect employee job satisfaction, the strongest factors are those with intrinsic value, as opposed to those with extrinsic value. While extrinsic rewards can confer short-term satisfaction on the part of employees, the benefit is generally transient and ultimately forgotten. The effect of intrinsic rewards, however, can last a lifetime.

Examples of extrinsic rewards are such things as giving an employee a raise, or naming her employee of the month. The giving of Christmas bonuses is a great example of how the positive effect of extrinsic rewards tends to attenuate over time. Many firms make a point of giving out Christmas bonuses to their employees every year. For a new employee, this can be quite an exciting event. The surprise of the reward, coupled with its size, can have a very positive effect on an employee. However, as years go by, the Christmas bonus loses its intended effect on the employee. Instead of being pleasantly surprised by the bonus, the long-term employee takes the bonus for granted—expecting it just as he expects his paycheck every other week. Heaven forbid that the company should decide, due to unfavorable market conditions for example, to cut or withhold the traditional bonus—that act becomes a tremendous *de*-motivator—tantamount to giving the employee a demotion or cutting his pay.

Intrinsic rewards include the satisfaction that comes with having done a job well and to the best of our abilities, and gaining the respect of our peers and superiors. While extrinsic rewards are conferred from without, intrinsic rewards are granted from within. The employee who has a high level of intrinsic satisfaction with his or her job is not dependent on receiving extrinsic rewards to maintain his or her job satisfaction. As long as the employee feels that his opinion and abilities are respected, that he is making a meaningful contribution to the organization, and that he is being treated fairly, it is likely that he will be a satisfied employee. Sure, raises, bonuses and such are satisfying, and a measure of management's commitment to its employees, but they are not the ultimate determinants of an employee's attitude while he or she is on the job.

So, how can we maximize our employees' intrinsic values and thereby increase their satisfaction, productivity, and effectiveness? One of the easiest ways to do so is by including your employees as valued and fully contributing participants in your organization's meetings. Inclusion builds an employee's sense of self-worth, while exclusion destroys it. No matter how many extrinsic rewards an employer may throw at an employee, if the employer does not truly value the abilities and opinions of the employee, then you can be sure that she will be dissatisfied with both her job and with her employer.

> There is no creature whose inward being is so strong that it is not greatly determined by what lies outside it.
>
> —George Eliot

So, why do satisfied employees give a firm a competitive advantage? It all comes down to dollars and cents. To begin, satisfied employees tend to work to further a company's goals rather than work against them. We all know how one dissatisfied employee can negatively affect the production of an entire work unit. If an employee has been wronged by an employer, other employees will jump to his defense. Before you know it, the employees will spend more time commiserating with the wronged employee than they spend doing their jobs. This can only lead to decreased productivity. Satisfied employees, on the other hand, are willing to go the extra mile to get the job done—not just completed, but done to the best of their abilities.

Employee turnover can be very expensive to a firm. While the cost of employee turnover averages $10,000 per position, in some companies and for some positions, this figure can approach $200,000.[6] As the employee rises in the hierarchy of the organization, the cost gets higher and higher. It is our experience that employees lacking in intrinsic job satisfaction tend to seek out employers who offer the potential of greater intrinsic reward. You can often judge the health of an organization by looking at its turnover statistics. Companies with low turnover rates generally value their employees, while companies with high turnover rates think about their bottom lines first and their employees a distant second.

In many cases, employees who have been ignored by the organization will simply drop out. Absenteeism increases, productivity decreases. This can go on for years and, unless someone makes some effort to make the employee a full-fledged member of the organization, the employee will become a drag on it.

Clearly, satisfied employees can be more efficient and more productive than dissatisfied employees. In many cases, all it takes for an employer to create a satisfied employee is to show the employee that he is an important and valued part of the team. Including employees as participants in meetings is one of the easiest ways that a manager can show an employee that the organization values his input and opinions.

The employer who makes the effort to include employees in meetings, and thereby increase their intrinsic value, will build a workforce that is lower cost, more loyal, and harder working than the employer who neglects this vital area of personnel management. The next time you conduct a meeting, don't be in too much of a hurry to consider the contributions that can be made by your staff. Sure—you could probably solve the problem by yourself—but allowing your employees to have a say in the direction of the organization will pay off handsomely at the bottom line.

## HOW TO TAP THE FULL POTENTIAL OF THE ORGANIZATION

The standard decision model is not the two- or three-hour meeting that leads to some momentous decision or new direction for the organization. Typically, the average business meeting leads to small decisions that are made over a long period of time. Eventually, the net effect of these small decisions a significant change in organizational policy or direction. The fact that the small decisions seem relatively minor compared to the larger ones makes them no less important to those involved in the decision making process. In fact, the individuals involved will typically be as emotionally invested in small decisions as they are in the large decisions because small decisions provide a convenient vehicle to demonstrate their expertise and experience.

We're sure that you would agree that it is important to involve employees in the decision-making process. Perhaps not for *every* decision, but at least for major decisions. It is critical when involving members of your organization in the decision-making process that you be perfectly clear in describing your expectations of the role that the participants will play.

If the group is going to be empowered with the authority to make and implement a decision, then clearly communicate that fact, and then be sure to honor it—regardless of the ultimate outcome of the meeting. If, however, the group will be making a recommendation only, and you will be making the final decision based on that recommendation, then be absolutely sure that you state that expectation to the group before the meeting starts. All too often, a leader will solicit a group's input, only to quickly discard it when it doesn't perfectly fit the leader's expectations. By raising the expectations of a group that is meeting to solve a problem and then discounting that group's recommendations, a leader almost guarantees that morale in the group will decrease, and dissension in the group will increase.

To ensure that meetings result in the most positive results possible, be sure to clearly set forth the decision-sharing role of the meeting participants when soliciting the involvement of co-workers in the decision-making process. The following true story took place at a recent off-site management meeting. The goals of the meeting were to develop mission and vision statements for the organization. At the beginning of the meeting, the participants were told that their task was to spend the day working on a list of key elements that would be made a part of the new mission and vision statements. The meeting leader, when describing the task before the group, left everyone with the clear impression that their input would form the basis of the mission and vision statements.

Excited by the prospect of making a real and lasting impact on the organization, the managers diligently went about the process of brainstorming, discussing and, in some cases, heatedly arguing their cases for particular goal statements. Some of the resultant mission and vision goal statements were truly innovative, others were not. Regardless of the outcome, however, the meeting process that the managers were going through was quickly cementing a team spirit within the group that many of the participants had never felt before. Things were going so well that the group sent out for lunch so that they could continue the brainstorming process uninterrupted.

At the end of the day, the management team completed their task. It had not been easy, but finally the team was satisfied with the new mission and vision statements. Pride and the feeling of a job well done radiated around the room. Unfortunately, this newfound team spirit was quickly shattered when the group leader got up to speak. He thanked everyone for pitching in, and then let the participants know in no uncertain terms that, ultimately, the final decision of the mission and vision statements rested with him. While he would consider the recommendations of the managers in the final versions of the statements, he had already developed some ideas of his own that he planned to use.

You can probably predict the reaction of the managers who participated in the meeting. The participants felt that they had been betrayed by their leader, and that neither their dedication nor their ideas were appreciated. As the managers who participated in the meeting spread the word among their co-workers, the organization's leadership was deemed to be decreasingly credible to proponents of employee empowerment and participation. The organization's leadership talked a big story about empowering individuals to make their own decisions but, when it really counted, leadership failed to follow through. Morale within the management team plummeted—affecting their subordinates, their co-workers, and even their customers. Cohesiveness within work groups and commitment to the organization decreased, and some of the managers began to actively subvert the decisions of the organization's leadership.

Examples like the above occur in organizations with surprising frequency. At times, the reasons for this miscommunication are inadvertent, such as management or environmental changes that are difficult to predict, or the manager who intends to involve subordinates but does so after the fact.

In other cases, the reason for miscommunication is intentional. Some managers simply distrust their employees and are afraid to involve them in any sort of decision-making process. The manager may short-circuit the participative process by changing group goals in midstream, taking credit for the group's recommendations, or ignoring the group's recommendations altogether. Of course, employees can easily see through these charades. The amount of loss to an organization due to subversion of the participative process, both in financial and in personnel terms, is incalculable.

Due to the increasing demands on our schedules, meetings are the only means for many of us to conduct face-to-face communication with our co-workers. In these days of modular offices, computer mail, voice mail, and fax machines, you can virtually conduct an entire day's business without directly contacting another living soul.

As a result, more and more people in business are feeling increasingly disenfranchised from their employers and from their co-workers. It's much easier to be uncooperative with a co-worker who approaches you via computer mail than it is to a co-worker who asks you for help in person. It's much easier to sabotage the efforts of an employer whom an employee sees as a faceless entity without a soul, than as an organization that takes a real, personal interest in all its employees.

Meetings provide the personal, one-on-one contact with our co-workers that we all need to thrive in an organization. Meetings also help to provide a sense of belonging for the participants. In some organizations, employee input or suggestions are not solicited except for when the employees participate in meetings. In such companies, meetings provide the only sanctioned channel of communication between employees and management, making them especially precious for the proper functioning of the organization.

Meetings are also more important than ever as a tool for managing change. Just as the pace of change in our society has accelerated, so has the velocity of change accelerated within our organizations. Businesses are microcosms of the world around them. While many businesses have their own unique opportunities, problems, and challenges, they closely mirror successes or failures of society. The better we are able to manage our diverse base of employees, the better able we will be to respond to changes in the marketplace.

## Chapter 9

# The Leading Edge of Meetings

**Objectives:**

- To define *empowerment,* and to explore the reasons why organizations are doing it, and employees are demanding it.
- To describe participative management techniques, such as quality circles and self-managed work teams.
- To explore the new wave of electronic meetings and computer-decision support systems.

While the basic reasons for having meetings have changed little over the years, the ways that we conduct them have changed dramatically. After years of a strict hierarchical management style, American business has begun a serious love affair with participatory decision making. Defined as pushing authority—and responsibility—farther down in the organization, empowerment is the goal of many organizations today. The demands of the market for increased product quality and decreased costs of production and operation, accompanied by an increasingly demanding workforce, have led to widespread experimentation with participative systems, such as quality circles and self-managing work teams. All participative management systems are, by nature, heavily dependent on meetings to function.

Recent strides in technology have led to a wide variety of meeting innovations, from teleconferencing, which allows meetings to be conducted with participants in different cities, states, or countries; to computer-aided meetings where participants interact anonymously through computer terminals; to decision-making computer software, which automates the entire meeting process, making human participation beyond the initial programming of the basic system unnecessary.

Regardless of how participatory, or how technology laden meetings become in the future, they are unlikely to ever become obsolete. If anything, as the marketplace becomes more competitive and communication systems become even faster than they are today, we will find ourselves meeting more than ever. Perhaps the structure, timing, and players will be different, but the concept of meeting face-to-face with others will likely remain viable well into the future. If we want to keep up with the changes to come, we have to learn and sharpen our meeting skills now.

## EMPLOYEE EMPOWERMENT

Although we have all heard a lot about employee empowerment, relatively few of us have actually experienced it. What exactly *is* this thing called empowerment, and what does it have to do with us? Back in the golden age of American business, empowerment applied generally to the owners of the corporation, not to the workers. Managers decided, and workers performed. It was a simple system that seemed to work just fine for us. The world clamored for our products, and we reigned supreme.

However, out of the ashes of World War II, other nations were laying foundations for businesses that would eventually rival, and in some cases surpass, our dominance of world markets. While the quality of our products declined in recent decades, the Germans built a strong reputation for precision-engineered, high-quality goods. During the same period, the Japanese went from being the laughing stock of the world to becoming an economic powerhouse. Both Germany and Japan built their businesses on a strong foundation of employee participation in basic business decisions—the Germans through the close partnership of corporations and trade unions, and the Japanese through social mechanisms such as quality circles.

Empowerment is nothing more than giving all employees a real voice in an organization's decision-making processes. Typical American businesses are all built on the same model: a large mass of relatively low-paid workers, who have little voice in the day-to-day operation of the business, and a small clique of relatively high-paid managers, who exercise control over the workers and most every substantive decision that affects them or the company. The main reason that managers are typically so protective of their right to control the organization is because the ability to control and direct others is what justifies their high salaries. Absent that, most managers would have a difficult time holding their own with their co-workers.

So why empowerment? Why now? It's no secret that American industry is in decline. Just as every empire before this one has reached its apex and then slowly slid into obscurity, so too has American industry found itself on the far side of its apex, watching from the sidelines as the vigorous new economic powers erupt all over the globe. As the Germans and Japanese were busy learning how to produce long-lasting, high-quality, functional products, we grew complacent, allowing our quality standards to fall precipitously. This doesn't mean we will never recapture more than mere shadows of our former glory. Indeed, many empires wax and wane, only to wax again, before they finally set into the sea.

> It is the nature of men to be bound by the benefits
> they confer as much as by those they receive.
>
> —Machiavelli

Empowerment is catching on because we know we need
to be more competitive, and we hope that, by emulating
the models of our most successful competitors, we will at
least keep up with them. The only problem is that, while a
lot of American companies talk about empowerment, very
few really practice it. Decisions are still made by small
groups of managers at the tops of the organizational pyra-
mids. Old habits die hard, and none so hard as the rigid,
hierarchical control of the vast majority of America's workforce by the fortunate few who wield the reins of power.

Most organizations that try to empower their workers
do so, not out of concern for the welfare of employees, but
for somewhat less altruistic reasons. The hope is that an
empowered employee will be a happy employee. And a
happy employee will presumably be a more productive
employee. The problem is that, if management does not
follow up the fanfare and big talk about employee empowerment with meaningful, widespread, and permanent organizational transformations, the real result will not be a
happy and productive workforce, but a disenchanted, disgruntled, and increasingly disillusioned workforce.

For all of our recent enthrallment with participatory
management systems, it is not clear that the results have
been substantially or uniformly better than the results we
saw from the old system of hierarchical decision making.
Many surveys have been conducted to measure the expected improvements in results that should accompany
participative decision making, but, to date, the results have
been inconclusive. In some cases, the implementation of

participative decision making in organizations has led to measurable improvements. In other cases, implementation has not led to any measurable improvements.

Regardless of the uncertainty of the outcomes, for most organizations, there are enough anecdotal instances of successful implementation of participative decision making in Fortune 500 corporations to maintain the interest of a large cross-section of American management. Whether or not participative decision making results in significant increases in productivity, once the majority of American workers get a taste for it, it is unlikely that they will readily allow a return to the old system of strict, hierarchical management.

## QUALITY CIRCLES

Quality circles were the first significant attempt at importing a successful model of Japanese participative decision making into an American industrial setting. As with participative decision making in general, the results have been mixed. Some companies, including AT&T, Westinghouse, Ford, and Honeywell, have reported phenomenal gains in revenue, productivity, and profitability. Other firms have abandoned quality circles after only a relatively short period of time.

A quality circle is a group of employees who meet on a regular basis to make recommendations for organizational improvements. The group is comprised of ten or so volunteer members; a leader who may or may not be a manager, supervisor, or regular worker; and a trained facilitator. An important point that distinguishes quality circles from other forms of participatory management systems is that the authority of quality circles is limited to recommending changes. In organizations that employ quality circles, management generally determines the overall scope of what the quality circles are allowed to address and makes the ultimate decision as to whether the recommendations of the quality circles will be implemented or ignored.

From an organizational point of view, the implementation of quality circles is a relatively painless way to introduce some form of participative decision making to an organization. Since management reserves its prerogative to accept or reject the recommendations of the quality circles, the basic organizational structures and procedures can remain in place. And, if management *does* make a point of implementing the recommendations of the organization's quality circles, employee morale is sure to improve for those employees who have successfully participated in the team process.

The meetings that are so important to the proper implementation of quality circles, and other similar programs such as total quality management or total quality leadership, are with few exceptions no different than the regular business meetings we have discussed throughout this book. Although they almost always are guided by well-trained facilitators, quality circle meetings are subject to the same problems and pitfalls as any other business meeting. While much of the responsibility for keeping the meeting running on an even keel is assumed by the facilitator, the quality circle leader and participants still must make a conscious effort to take an active role in the management of the quality circle meetings.

In many cases, due to no fault of the meeting process, quality circles and similar marginally participative decision-making systems have failed or have been scrapped by their organizations. We Americans tend to be very impatient when it comes to getting results in business (or anywhere else, for that matter!). We want results, and we want them now! If we can't see immediate results from our efforts, we quickly grow impatient, and either cancel our implementation or seek out some other quick fix that looks a little greener from our side of the fence.

Quality circles are not the instant panacea that many of us hoped for when we decided to implement them. Like any other management technique, it takes time and persistence to reap the benefits of what we have sown. Too many firms give up too soon. It has taken Hybritech, a large Southern California biotechnology firm, five years to get its quality program, dubbed *Team Excellence* off the ground and functioning efficiently and effectively. The first couple of years, devoted to program design, personnel training, and implementation, were marked with dramatic stops and starts. There were many points along the way where it would have been very easy for management to give up. To its credit, Hybritech stuck with it, and now they have a program in place that is a model of effectiveness, and one that other companies are falling all over themselves to emulate.

In the long run, it's hard to say what will come of quality circles and similar programs. To work, they require a real and lasting commitment from management to support their implementation and continued viability. Unfortunately, it is quite possible that most of us will go back to business as usual once the novelty of the program wears off and employee interest begins to wane. And, like the other management fads that preceded this one, quality circles will find themselves on the junk heap of management techniques that didn't stand the test of time.

## SELF-MANAGING WORK TEAMS

Unlike quality circles, which tend to represent nothing more than a Band-Aid approach to employee empowerment, self-managing work teams (SMWTs) represent major surgery. In quality circles, and other *total quality*-type techniques, employee teams are generally empowered only to make recommendations in specific areas that management has sanctioned. And, although the team may be called upon to implement their recommendations, they can do so only with the explicit approval of management.

Self-managing work teams, however, are a giant step beyond these lesser attempts at employee empowerment. SMWTs are not only responsible for selecting the scope of work and planning and organizing to get the work done, they are also responsible for the selection of group members and supervision of the members of the group. Like quality circles, however, self-managed work teams rely very heavily on regular meetings of team members to function properly.

In 1974, Peter Drucker wrote in the *Harvard Business Review* that: "Whereas team design has traditionally been considered applicable only to short-lived, transitory, exceptional taskforce assignments, it is equally applicable to some permanent needs, especially to the top-management and innovating tasks."[1] Clearly, times have changed, and the team concept has proved itself to be a workable long-term solution to the needs of many organizations.

The story of Keithley Instruments is typical of the success that can be attained through the deliberate and concerted efforts of self-managed work teams. Keithley Instruments is an Ohio designer and manufacturer of complex electronic measurement instruments. In 1979, Keithley management determined that something would have to be done to stem the tide that was rising to ever-higher levels, and to reverse the decline in manufacturing productivity that became more evident with each passing month. Based on a complete review of company operations, Keithley's vice president of manufacturing decided to implement self-managing work teams.

Keithley Instruments restructured its manufacturing operations from a standard assembly line approach to a work team approach. Instead of the old way of individual task specialization, each team, made up of twelve members on average, was assigned the initiation, completion, and inspection of the complete instrument—not just a single subsystem. Eventually, twelve teams were assembled, and *all* team members were provided thorough training in team procedures, team goals, team building skills, production methods, products, and costs. Team supervisors were given additional training in counseling, motivation, and other traditional supervision skills. In addition to this training, each team was provided with complete market and development information.

As a result of the conversion to self-managed work teams, Keithley Instruments was able to :

❑ Double productivity.
❑ Improve product quality by 15 percent.
❑ Decrease absenteeism by 80 percent.
❑ Significantly increase the levels of reported job satisfaction by employees and supervisors.

Still, SMWTs are not for every organization. For self-managed work teams to work, not only does management have to make a radical shift from its standard, hierarchical paradigms, but the members of self-managed work teams must have the ability and commitment to take responsibility for their own actions. Here are some of the strengths and weaknesses of SMWTs, and some indicators of when they will be most likely to succeed in an organization.

### *The Strengths of Self-Managing Work Teams*

The strengths of self-managing work teams include better decision making, faster decision making, and a greater degree of employee development. Those employees closest to a job or task tend to know best the needs and problems associated with the position. As a result, the probability of better decision making increases when done by self-managing work teams.

Not only does the potential exist for decisions to be better, but they can be made faster as well, again since team members are closest to the problems and to each other. This results in a minimal amount of lag time due to convoluted, multi-layered communication channels or the need to get approval from others in the organization.

And more responsibility for a greater number and type of decisions serves to quickly develop the managerial skills of *all* team members. This is an important advantage in an age where the labor pool that is decreasingly skilled, and increasingly undereducated. Organizations will increasingly need to fully develop their management talent from within, and SMWTs are a great way to do so.

## Limits of Self-Managing Work Teams

On the down side, the limitations of self-managing work teams include the difficulty of getting them going, a high level of required maintenance, and problems with integration into more traditional organizational structures. As might be expected, the implementation of self-managing work teams requires a lot of nurturing by an organization's management. Group members must be instructed in team skills as well as in the new technical skills required to be a full-fledged member of the work team. Supervisors have to be taught how to let go of years of authoritarian supervision skills and instead utilize coaching and other effective team management skills.

And, once the teams are up and running, management can't just walk away to turn its attention to other, more pressing matters. The implementation of self-managing work teams requires the ongoing efforts of management to ensure their success. Not only must management continue to provide a large amount of high-quality information, for example, but management must not undermine the efforts of the SMWTs by taking actions that are contrary to their full and unfettered operation.

A final limitation is that, because they are so dramatically different from the status quo, self-managed work teams cannot survive very long within traditional organizational frameworks. The deviation from the accepted hierarchy, the differing needs and accountabilities, make the SMWT form of organization a direct threat to the larger, traditional structure of most companies. In most cases, this has led to the abandonment of the self-managed work team format or a move to shift the entire organization to a related organizational style.

## *Terms of Effectiveness*

The most effective conditions under which self-managed work teams are incorporated are when this form of decentralization fits the organization's business strategy for the market in which it competes. This is also the case when the external environment is quickly or constantly changing so that the self-managed work team's size and flexibility allow it a distinctive advantage over the more traditional organizational structures of competing organizations. Since, increasingly, the ability to compete in time is a significant competitive advantage, this is a major advantage for the SMWT unit.

---

Time is a more critical competitive yardstick than traditional financial measurements.

—George Stalk

Of course, for self-managed work teams to thrive, there must also be a willingness on the part of management to embark on an extensive program of constant training and to reward participants for the new skills they learn and apply on the job. A self-managed work team program implemented without this critical support by management is doomed to failure before it starts.

The least effective conditions for implementation include highly structured, large operations that benefit from standardization of practice and efficiency of scale. In such cases, there would be limited advantages to using SMWTs, and the likelihood of disadvantages would increase. Individual work groups would be likely to deviate from the organizational standards, and the efficiency of scale would be lost.

In summary, the benefits of self-managed work teams can be substantial. Greater participation in setting goals leads to greater commitment to achieving those goals and, as a result, to higher performance. And, in general, employee morale and motivation is improved as the responsibility for actions is delegated farther down the organizational chain of command, along with the tools to perform well.

## ELECTRONIC MEETINGS

It used to be that, if you wanted to meet with associates who worked in cities, states, or countries other than your own, one or all of you would have to travel to a single site to have the meeting. While there is still plenty of business travel for just that very reason, more and more, electronic meetings are taking over the good old-fashioned face-to-face meetings that were such an important part of doing business for such a long time. While living, breathing human beings are still the basis for group interaction in electronic meetings, it is likely that advances in computers, decision-making software, and artificial intelligence will to some degree eventually supplant much of the current need for human interaction in the meeting process.

We are all by now familiar with teleconferencing, an electronic system that allows us to link several telephone instruments into an interactive real-time meeting network. A fairly recent innovation, teleconferencing can be used, for example, to call a meeting of three business people located on three different continents, or it can be used to link three people on three different floors of a building.

With the introduction of teleconferencing, no longer do business people have to physically be in the same room together to hold a real-time conference. And, with the introduction of speakerphones, which can broadcast the output of a telephone to an entire room, or even an entire auditorium full of meeting participants, and pick up the input of internal or external microphones, the number of people who could participate in a teleconference skyrocketed.

While teleconferences are a convenient way to meet and can help to stretch a company's travel budget a lot farther, teleconferencing does have its downside. To begin, it can be very difficult to exactly schedule and then execute a teleconference. Despite our best efforts to be in our seat, awaiting the conference call at the appointed hour, it is often the case that we are drawn away from our desks right at the moment that the teleconferencing call comes through. And, of course, if we're not there to accept the call, then the conference can't be initiated and the meeting leader will have to try to put the pieces together again later. Also, if by some chance you're on the phone when the teleconferencing call comes through, your part in the meeting will be nothing more than a busy signal.

One other problem with teleconferencing is that, since the meeting is strictly an audio experience, and not a visual one, we miss out on the nonverbal communication channels that a face-to-face meeting offers, and we are unable to utilize visual aids such as white boards, flip charts, or view graphs in our meetings. As we all know, the non-verbal and visual components of our communication with others can be very important to our overall understanding of an issue. Absent these important information streams, meetings can be more difficult and more troublesome than normal, face-to-face meetings.

The next step up from teleconferencing is videoconferencing. The basic idea is the same as teleconferencing, but with the addition of the visual component of meetings that is so important when we personally interact with another person on a face-to-face basis. To date, however, videoconferencing has remained a prohibitively expensive proposition for most organizations. Just a few years ago, the computer chip set required to transfer video data across telephone lines, called the codec, cost one quarter of a million dollars. This didn't include the price for video cameras and the other accessories needed to make the videoconferencing system work. Today, complete video-room systems including the codec and a video camera start at around $20,000—still a little pricey for most firms.

As with most computer-based equipment, the move is toward much smaller, desktop based systems. Roger Redmond, managing director of brokers Piper, Jaffrey & Hopwood, Inc., was quoted in a *Business Week* article as saying, "I think there will be a large market for these [desktop] systems, but it is a little way off."[2] Clearly, until these systems become much more affordable, it will be some time before videoconferencing becomes commonplace.

Finally, there are computer-aided meetings. In this form of electronic meeting, up to 50 participants sit around a u-shaped table—empty except for 50 personal computers. A sophisticated computer processor gathers the input of each participant, categorizes it, and displays it on a large projection screen. The interesting aspect about computer-aided meetings is that, since the inputs are anonymous, participants become brutally honest, and much braver than they would be in a typical face-to-face meeting situation.

According to *Business Week* magazine, computer-aided meetings get high marks for efficiency and for cutting through the chitchat and digression that often accompanies more conventional business meetings. According to the article, a study by IBM and the University of Arizona found that computer-aided meetings are 55 percent faster than conventional meetings. Meetings that formerly took several days to complete can be completed in mere hours using computer-aided techniques.[3]

Regardless of all these technological advances, most people agree there is still no substitute for face-to-face interaction. The secret is in using advances in computer technology as adjuncts to your meetings, not as substitutes for them. As our world becomes increasingly impersonal, it is even more important that we retain as much humanity in our business dealings as possible. Despite the pressures to rush everything and to take the quickest path between two points, we will all be better off for taking the time to relate to each other on a one-on-one basis, to revel in our humanity, and to occasionally stop to smell the roses.

## DECISION SUPPORT SYSTEMS

Some day, decision-making meetings may be obsolete. Recent advances in computer hardware, computer software, fuzzy logic, and artificial intelligence have brought this day closer to fruition. Instead of calling a meeting to present options and make decisions, the meeting of the future will take place instantly, and silently, on your desktop.

The basis for most decision support software is a sophisticated system of weighting of key decision criteria. If, for example, you are planning to build a new fast-food franchise in Dallas, you might have three key criteria in your decision-making process: rent, projected sales, and area demographics. You would then assign weights to each of the criteria: say, 30 percent for rent, 50 percent for projected sales, and 20 percent for area demographics. After inputting your criteria and your weightings for each criteria, you can then take a long list of candidate locations, input the pertinent data into the computer, and receive a summarized, rank ordered scoring of the candidate sites for your review. While a real example would likely be much more complex, with many more factors, it would still work in this fashion.

The advantages of such systems are that they avoid the emotion that often accompanies important or highly charged deliberations, and they can quickly and accurately sort through the different factors contributing to a decision. Of course, the utility of such programs is limited to the information that is input to the system. If the data is incomplete or incorrect, the results will necessarily be poor. As with any other computer program, if you put garbage in, you will definitely get garbage out.

Again, as with electronic meetings, there is still no substitute for the humanness of meeting or making decisions. There is no computer on earth that can even begin to rival the human mind. Until there is, decision support systems should be used only as an aid in the decision-making process, not as a replacement for it.

## Chapter 10

# Better Business Meetings

A s we have seen, despite recent advances in technology and office automation, meetings are more necessary than ever. While the form of meetings may change, with computers and digital voice and image transmission becoming more prevalent as meeting tools, the reasons for having meetings will likely remain the same as they always have been. We meet to share information within an organization. We meet to train our co-workers. We meet to study problems and make recommendations. We meet to make decisions. We meet to socialize with our peers and associates—to share in our successes and console each other in our failures.

The reason that meetings will never be replaced is that meetings are a uniquely human activity and, as long as we still carry an ounce of humanity within us, we will always meet with each other to achieve our goals. We are social animals. No amount of fancy electronic wizardry or high-tech, computer-based, decision-making software or hardware will ever change that fundamental fact.

We have seen the tremendous, real costs to an organization due to ineffective meetings. This cost, which few of us acknowledge much less take steps to prevent, can be an enormous drain on the profitability of a corporation. For a large corporation, the time lost in meetings by managers alone can be staggering—easily numbering in the tens of thousands of hours, and totaling in the tens of millions of dollars. With most meetings only averaging 47 percent efficiency, there is clearly room for improvement.

We are faced with two choices: We can either ignore the problem and fail to stem the flow of red ink from this obvious source of waste, or we can take action to make our meetings better and thereby improve the efficiency and profitability of our organizations. It's easy enough to ignore the problem. That's what most of us have been doing all along. We have all suffered through far too many wasted hours in far too many wasted meetings. We just tend to take it for granted that our job descriptions include a certain amount of this wasted time and drudgery—especially as we rise up in the ranks of management.

The Power Dynamics method developed by the authors is an easy to apply and effective way to take action to make business meetings better. When you commit to using the techniques we have described herein, you make a pledge to take an active and responsible role as a meeting leader or meeting participant. No longer can you sit on the sidelines and simply warm the bench. If you decide to use the methods described in this book, you will become a critical player in the meeting process. And, as you introduce your co-workers and associates to these techniques, you will become an important agent for change in your organization and for increased organizational efficiency and effectiveness.

The easiest and often the most effective way to make business meetings better is to question the reason why the meeting is being held and the need for your attendance. How often do you personally refuse an invitation to a meeting? No, we're not talking about those times when you already have a meeting scheduled and the invitation conflicts. If you are like most of us, you probably simply honor the request, duly note it in your calendar, and attend when the time comes. While it is unrealistic to expect to avoid regularly scheduled meetings such as staff meetings, you should take the time to seriously consider the need to attend every other meeting that you are invited to attend.

Once you make a habit of questioning the need for your attendance, you will be pleasantly surprised at how often you can solve the issue by a phone call or simple one-on-one meeting. Not every issue requires a full-blown meeting to solve, and not every piece of news or information warrants calling all employees together to transmit it. And, once you start missing some of the meetings that would have normally occupied your valuable time, you will be pleasantly surprised at how much time becomes available to take care of your routine business tasks, and how much less demand there is on your personal time.

It's your choice. You can either continue with the status quo, or you can decide to make a real and lasting change in your work life, and in your organization. In this book, we have given you all the tools you need to make your business meetings better. These techniques have worked for us, and they have worked for our associates. We know they will work for you. Please write to us in care of the publisher, and tell us about your successes. We look forward to hearing from you.

# ENDNOTES

## Chapter 1

[1]Calonius, Erik, "How Top Managers Manage Their Time," *Fortune* (June 1990).

## Chapter 2

[1]O'Reilly, Brian, "John Sculley on Sabbatical," *Fortune* (March 1989).

## Chapter 3

[1]Calonius, Erik, "How Top Managers Manage Their Time," *Fortune* (June 1990).

## Chapter 4

[1]Calonius, Erik, "How Top Managers Manage Their Time," *Fortune* (June 1990).

## Chapter 5

[1]Drucker, Peter F., *Management: Tasks, Responsibilities, Practices* (New York: Harper and Row, 1974).

## Chapter 6

[1]Goldhammer, E., and E. Shils, "Types of Power and Status," *American Journal of Sociology* 45 (1939).

## Chapter 7

[1]Calonius, Erik, "How Top Managers Manage Their Time," *Fortune* (June 1990).

## Chapter 8

[1]Feminist Majority Foundation, "Empowering Women in Business," *Feminist Majority Foundation* (1991).

[2]Hoffman, Mark S., Editor. *The World Almanac and Book of Facts 1993* (New York: Pharos Books, 1992).

[3]Catalyst, *Women in Corporate Management: Results of a Catalyst Survey* (New York: Catalyst, 1990).

[4]Cox, Taylor, Jr. and Stella M. Nkomo, "Differential Performance Appraisal Criteria: A Field Study of Black and White Managers," *Group & Organization Studies* (March–June 1986).

[5]Peters, Tom, *Liberation Management* (New York: Knopf, 1992).

[6]Hinrichs, John R., "Commitment Ties to the Bottom Line," *Human Resource Magazine* (April 1991).

**Chapter 9**

[1]Drucker, Peter F., "New Templates for Today's Organizations," *The Harvard Business Review* (January–February 1974).

[2]Bhargava, Sunita Wadekar, and Peter Coy, "Video-Screen Meetings: Still Out of Sight," *Business Week* (November 1991).

[3]Bartimo, Jim, "At These Shouting Matches, No One Says a Word," *Business Week* (June 1990).

# Index

**A**

Agenda, 10, 36, 39–40, 42–45,
    115–17, 124–25
  leadership skills, 80
Authoritarian organization style,
    131

**B**

Bacon, Sir Francis, 96
Baker, James, 63
Bartimo, Jim, 175
Behavioral change, 57
Bhargava, Sunita Wadekar, 175
Brainstorming meeting, 37–38, 74

**C**

Calonius, Erik, 174
Collins, Churton, 56
Computer-aided meetings, 168–69
Corporate demographics, 130
  nature of diversity, 134
Cox, Taylor, Jr., 174
Coy, Peter, 175
Cultural factors in international
    meetings, 138–39
Cutler, Laurel, 31

**D**

Decision-making process
  chain of command style, 142–44
  decision support systems, 169
  employee participation, 133,
    145–46, 151–54
  use of meetings, 134
Decision support systems, 169
Dissent, promotion of, 76–77,
    81–82
Drucker, Peter, 76, 162, 174, 175

**E**

Electronic meetings, 166
Eliot, George, 149
Employee empowerment, 156–59

**G**

Gender-specific traits, 106
  cultural differences, 136
Goals of meeting, 30–31
Goldhammer, E., 107
Grace, J. Peter, 3
Group meetings, 30
Groupthink, 63–69

## H

Hybritech, 161
Harkness, Richard, 88
Hinrichs, John R., 174
Hoffman, Mark S., 174

## I–J

Inclusionary participative
    management, 145
Job satisfaction, 147–50
    rewards, 147–48
Jowett, Benjamin, 146

## K–L

Keithley Instruments, 162–63
Kipling, Rudyard, 135
Leadership
    authoritarian style, 71–74
    building team, 93–94
    controlling domination by
        participants, 85, 120
    encouraging input, 83–85
    myths of, 75–79
    participants as leaders, 96–98
    participative style, 72–75
    preparedness for meetings,
        62–63
    sharing leadership position,
        58–59, 78–79
    skills, 79–83
    talking less, listening more,
        59–60
Listening as participant skill, 98

## M

Management: Tasks, Responsibilities,
    Practices (Drucker), 76
Meeting(s)

Meeting(s)—Cont.
    agenda, 10, 36, 39–40, 42–46
    basic reasons for, 2–9
        communication vehicles, 4,
            6–9
        competition, 3–4
        electronic, 166–69
        failure, reasons for
            apathetic members, 24–25
            costs, 18–20
            inefficient, unproductive,
                17–20
            lack of control of dominating
                participants, 21–24
            lack of preparation, 20
            too many meetings, 14–15
            too time consuming, 16–17,
                117–20
        goals of, 30–31, 115–17
        ground rules, 36–42
        how to have fewer meetings,
            45–49
        improvement, 172–73
        leadership; see Leadership
        mistakes to avoid; see Mistakes
        number of attendees, 31–34, 44,
            48
        participation; see Participation
            and Participative
            management
        rewarding truth-telling, 25–26
        scheduling, 34
Meeting facilitator, 60, 68
Meeting management
    concluding meetings, 67–69
    drawing out minority opinion,
        56
    leadership, 58–63
    mistakes; see Mistakes
    Power Dynamics method, 51–52
        changing group behavior,
            57–67
    talk time of participants, 52–55

Meeting participants; *see*
    Participation
Memorandum, 6–9
Mistakes, 112
    ambiguous results, 123–27
    domination by participant, 128
    getting off subject, 113
    key participants missing, 127
    lack of preparation, 120–23
    meeting too long, 117–20
    no goals or agenda, 115–17
Morale, 145
Multicultural work groups, 130


**N–O**

Nkomo, Stella, M., 174
O'Reilly, Brian, 174
Organizational vision statement,
    132


**P**

Participation, 95, 133, 145–46,
    151–54
    conflict resolution, 103–4
    contribution characteristics,
        107–9
    diplomatic approach to
        disagreements, 109–10
    domination, 99–101, 128–29
    influencing group, 105
    organization, 101
    participants as meeting leaders,
        96–98
    self-confidence of participants,
        102–3
Participative management, 132,
    155

Participative management,—*Cont.*
    employee empowerment,
        156–59
    leadership style, 72–75
    quality circles, 159–61
    reasons for development, 145
Peters, Tom, 143, 174
Power Dynamics method of
        meeting management, 51–52
    changing group behavior, 57–67
    feedback mechanisms and
        evaluation, 69–71
    improving meetings, 172
Preparing for meeting, 62–63
    premeeting exercises, 103
    prework, 140–41
Proust, Marcel, 113


**Q–R**

Quality circles, 159–61
Race and ethnic differences,
    137–38
Redmond, Roger, 168
Reward to employees, 147–48
Rotated presentations, 141


**S**

Sculley, John, 12
Self-managing work teams
        (SMWTs), 161–66
    limits, 164–65
    strengths, 163–64
    terms of effectiveness, 165–66
Shils, E., 107, 174
Smith, Sidney, 103
Staff meetings, 29, 31
Stalk, George, 15

**T**

Talk time of meeting participants,
52–55
distribution, 53
status of individual
determining, 55
Taylor, Henry, 124, 132
*Team Excellence*, 161
Teamwork, 82–83, 93–94
self-managing work teams,
161–66
Teleconferencing, 156, 167–68

**V–W**

Videoconferencing, 168
Williams, Jimmy, 118
Women
in executive positions, 130–135
gender-specific personality
traits, 106–7, 136
Work teams, 161–66

Other books of interest to you from Irwin *Professional Publishing* . . .

### SURVIVE INFORMATION OVERLOAD
### The 7 Best Ways to Manage Your Workload by Seeing the Big Picture
Kathryn Alesandrini

You'll discover how to use innovative techniques so you can manage information efficiently, prevent paper buildup, make meetings more effective, capture ideas, and organize thoughts for enhanced productivity. (225 pages)
ISBN:   1-55623-721-9

### UNLEASHING PRODUCTIVITY!
### Your Guide to Unlocking the Secrets of Super Performance
Richard Ott with Martin Sneed

This quick-read to becoming more creative, productive, and satisfied shows how to recognize and remove productivity barriers. Packed with tips, techniques, and ideas that show how to get the most from your workforce and yourself. (200 pages)
ISBN:   1-55623-931-9

Available at fine bookstores and libraries everywhere.

## 1. How did you find out about this Briefcase Book?

- ☐ Bookstore
- ☐ Advertisement
- ☐ Flyer
- ☐ Sales Rep
- ☐ Irwin Catalog
- ☐ Convention
- ☐ Other Catalog
- other _____

## 2. Was this book provided by your organization or did you purchase this book for yourself?

- ☐ individual purchase
- ☐ organizational purchase

## 3. Are you using this book as a part of a training program?

- ☐ yes  ☐ no

## 4. Did this book meet your expectations?

- ☐ yes  ☐ no

(please explain) _____

_____
_____
_____
_____

## 5. What other topics would you like to see addressed in this series?

*(Please list)*

_____
_____

## 6. ☐ *Please have a sales representative call me.*

*I am interested in:*

- ☐ bulk purchase discounts
- ☐ custom publishing

## 7. ☐ *Please send me a catalog of your products.*

_____
*Name*

_____
*Title*

_____
*Organization*

_____
*Address*

_____
*City, State, Zip*

_____
*Phone*

# BUSINESS REPLY MAIL

FIRST CLASS    PERMIT NO. 99    HOMEWOOD, IL

POSTAGE WILL BE PAID BY ADDRESSEE

## IRWIN

*Professional Publishing*

**Attn: Cindy Zigmund**
**1333 Burr Ridge Parkway**
**Burr Ridge, IL 60521-0081**